WILL THE GENTLEMAN YIELD?

WILL THE GENTLEMAN
YIELD?

★ The Congressional Record Humor Book ★

by Bill Hogan and Mike Hill

A Tilden Press Book

Ten Speed Press

1☉
TEN SPEED PRESS
P.O. Box 7123
Berkeley, California 94707

Cover design by Fifth Street Design
Text design by Jann Alexander
Phototypography by Chronicle Type & Design

Library of Congress Cataloging-in-Publication Data

Will the gentleman yield?

   Collection of extracts primarily from the
Congressional records.
   Includes index.
   1. United States—Politics and government—1945-
Anecdotes, facetiae, satire, etc. 2. United States.
Congress—Anecdotes, facetiae, satire. 3. Political
satire, American. I. Hogan, Bill, 1953-   . II. Hill,
Mike, 1953-   . III. Congressional records.
E839.5.W545 1987   328.73'00207   87-10203
ISBN 0-89815-215-1

Manufactured in the United States of America

1 2 3 4 5 6 7 8 9 0   —   91 90 89 88 87

For our parents

CONTENTS

ACKNOWLEDGMENTS

Every book has its share of toil and trouble, but this one has, from the beginning, been a genuine labor of love. Many of the people around us have helped make it so, and for that we consider ourselves especially lucky souls.

We must first of all acknowledge a certain debt to Senate Majority Leader Robert C. Byrd of West Virginia and former Senator S.I. Hayakawa of California, who, on September 8, 1978, unknowingly provided the initial inspiration for this book. We have met neither of them, but their off-the-cuff colloquy on the Senate floor that day (which appears on page 44 of this book) convinced us early on that the *Congressional Record* was a mother lode of humor. We have been trying to mine it ever since, and this book is the result.

Along the way, many friends, colleagues, and editors have provided us with help, encouragement, and inspiration. Among them: Tina Adler, Blair Austin, Reid Beddow, Ken Burns, Jim Dentzer (whose research and other assistance went way beyond the call of duty), Jim Eastwood, Anne Eisele, Henry Fortunato, Jojo Gragasin, Alan Green, Nick Kotz, David McCullough, Evan Roth, John Rosenberg, Bob Vasilak, and Lewis Wolfson.

As we went about compiling this book, many Capitol Hill staffers were especially courteous and kind to us. Listing them all here would be impossible. But we do wish to extend a special measure of appreciation to some of those who took the time to sift through files and buttonhole others in their offices with an eye toward providing us with fodder for our book. They include Bill Black, David Bryant, Dan Buck, Doug Cahn, Mary Ann Hatchitt, Elaine Lang, Cathy Noe, Carey Parker, Barbara Powe, and Diane Skvarla. Richard Baker and Don Ritchie of the Senate Historical Office helped us in innumerable ways, big and small. And Representative Andy Jacobs of Indiana, who is well-represented in this volume, was kind enough to sit down and talk with us.

We wish to thank a number of other persons for sharing leads, recollections, or clippings with us: Norman Black, Francis X. Gannon, George Hager, Margaret Shannon, and Terry Ware and Dan McIvery of the Government Printing Office. Yet our most profound appreciation goes to Joseph J. Allan of Hyattsville, Maryland, a reader of the *Congressional Record* for twenty-five years, who sent us an extensive list of citations compiled from his own clipping files. A good number of them appear in this book, including many we simply could not have found without his generous and unsolicited help.

Above all, we owe thanks to Joel Makower, a good friend, agent, and president of Tilden Press Inc. He shepherded this book from its infancy through completion with enthusiasm, grace, and good humor. And no writers could hope for a happier relationship with their publisher than we have had with Ten Speed Press—and, in particular, with Patti Breitman, Ten Speed's executive editor.

Finally, we wish to thank those members of Congress, past and present, who are represented in this book. They have given us one of the greatest gifts of all: laughter.

—B.H. and M.H.
June, 1987
Alexandria, Virginia

Mr. MIKVA. Mr. Speaker, will the gentleman yield?
Mr. HUNGATE. I have two more jokes.

—Reps. Abner J. Mikva (D-Ill.) and William L. Hungate (D-Mo.)
May 22, 1975

INTRODUCTION

I received a wire from a Congressman friend of mine who wants a copy of some fool thing that pertains to the bill that they are kidding about in Congress. He wants to read it into the *Congressional Record*.

I feel pretty good about that. That's the biggest praise that a humorist can have, is to get your stuff into the *Congressional Record*. Just think, my name will be right alongside all those other big humorists.

—Will Rogers

Will Rogers used to joke that he got a lot of his best material from the *Congressional Record*, and so it is with us.

For nearly a decade, we have been faithful readers of the *Congressional Record*. While it's not exactly the kind of thing either of us would feel comfortable volunteering in casual conversation—at a cocktail party, say—our fascination with this remarkable publication turned, some while back, into an addiction. We became *Congressional Record* junkies.

What got us hooked on the *Record*, really, was humor. The U.S. Congress conducts a fair amount of serious business, but there are times when it becomes, as Will Rogers put it, the "Capitol Comedy Co. of Washington, D.C." A shame, we thought, that no one had seen fit to expose the lighter side of Congress, at least as it has been captured over the years in the pages of the *Record*.

That is what we have attempted to do in Will the Gentleman Yield? We've collected material from dozens of Capitol Hill's top funny men and women, from reporters who have watched it all from ringside seats in the congressional press galleries, from the official historians of the Senate and House of Representatives, and, of course, from the pages of the *Record* itself. We've begged, borrowed, and photocopied from private collections. All told, we figure, we've rummaged through more than a half-million pages of the *Record* in search of the material that eventually found its way into this book.

Everything in the pages that follow—save for occasional introductions, annotations, and headings—is presented as it appeared in the *Congressional Record* or, in a few instances, its predecessors, the *Annals of Congress* and *The Congressional Globe*. While we generally have corrected misspellings and typographical errors, we thought it important to maintain the distinctive style of the *Record* in punctuation, capitalization, and so forth. (In a few instances, we've edited some rather long-winded entries to zero in on the humorous business at hand.) When it made sense to condense, we resorted to ellipses. Readers should rest assured, however, that we sought to be conservative in tinkering with text.

Although by law the *Congressional Record* is supposed to represent the "public proceedings of each House of Congress, as reported by the Official Reporters thereof," what readers see frequently isn't what actually was said. Members of Congress are allowed to fiddle with transcripts of their remarks—to add, subtract, or otherwise alter them—before they go to press. The consequence, of course, is that the *Record* is a little bit like a funhouse mirror. For this reason, we've not tried to distinguish between passages actually spoken and those simply inserted for the record, nor can we vouch for the accuracy of the accounts themselves. Complaints on that score should be sent directly to Congress itself.

Now, finally, we yield to our readers.

GUNS FIRE
CHICKENS
AT PLANES

All the News that Fits

GUNS FIRE
CHICKENS
AT PLANES

FOWL PLAY

Mr. BAKER. Mr. President, yesterday, while browsing through the New York Times, I came upon a story of major significance that I would now like to share with my colleagues. I am hopeful that this story is as comforting to them as it was to me. The story stated the following:

GUNS FIRE CHICKENS AT PLANES

LANGLEY, VA., June 8—Officials at Langley Air Force Base said today that a cannon that hurls dead chickens at airplanes at 700 miles an hour is helping to reduce accidents caused by jets hitting birds. Maj. Dennis Funnemark said the device, called a chicken gun, was a converted 20-foot cannon that shoots 4-pound chickens into engines, windshields and landing gear to determine how much damage such collisions can cause.

Mr. President, I must admit that my first reaction to this story was one of bitterness. I wondered why a special classified briefing had not been set up for Members of Congress on the new chicken gun, and I wondered if Secretary of Defense Weinberger was planning one. I was also surprised that the New York Times decided to run this story on the bottom of page A24, since this newest strategic development speaks directly to our Nation's safety, and might even change the focus of the defense budget debate.

I am sure that since reading the story yesterday, many Americans are trying to find out how far along the Soviet Union is with their deployment of the chicken gun, and how will our Minuteman, Midgetman, and Sparrow missiles get along with this new weapon, which I would personally like to call the Perdue missile. I am also trying to find out if the Navy is working with the Air Force on this project to develop one of their own missiles which would be, one assumes, a chicken of the sea.

These concerns notwithstanding, Mr. President, I want to congratulate the Air Force on their resourcefulness and attention to a most disturbing problem. Despite the fact that there will no doubt be those that will be skeptical of such research, I for one, see nothing more involved than a little "fowl" play.

Mr. President, I have no further need for my time.

—Sen. Howard H. Baker, Jr. (R-Tenn.)
June 10, 1983

THE EYES HAVE IT

Mr. STALLINGS. Mr. Speaker, I would like to take this opportunity to pay tribute to Mr. Gary Ball, a resident of my district in Idaho who recently has been named "Potato Man of the Year" by a national produce magazine. Mr. Ball has worked hard to promote our Idaho potatoes through his efforts on the National Potato Promotions Board, the National Potato Council, and in many other areas.

—Rep. Richard H. Stallings (D-Idaho)
February 6, 1986

THE NONCANDIDATE

Mr. HUGH SCOTT. Mr. President, the Presidential campaign of 1976, I suppose, will be interlaced with numerous declarations of candidacy, and in that regard I do not want to exclude any of my colleagues in this body. But a new switch appears when there seems to be more publicity about an announcement of noncandidacy than there is about announcements of candidacy.

I suggest that all of our colleagues who are not bitten by the Presidential bug can amass for themselves a certain amount of publicity by announcing consecutively that they are not candidates for the Presidency. I suggest that this be done on Friday, in order to get in the weekend papers. It offers an opportunity for a speech, some philosophical reflections on the state of the Union, and then the Senator's own contribution to the improvement of the state of the Union by his decision not to head it. This could well be a salutary proceeding. If necessary, we can set aside the morning hour for successive days for these announcements of noncandidacy.

Certainly, noncandidacy is important. Noncandidacy is news. Noncandidacy implies a certain spirit of sacrifice, a certain willingness to abase oneself below the peak or to situate oneself further down the slopes of Everest.

So I am in favor of noncandidacy. I think the more noncandidates we have, the better for the country. These are all eminent gentlemen and well qualified. Every one of them is admirably qualified to be a noncandidate. [Laughter.]

Mr. President, I yield back the remainder of my time.

—Sen. Hugh Scott (R-Pa.)
November 25, 1974

TERMS OF ENDUREMENT

Mr. HINSHAW. Mr. Speaker, under leave to extend my remarks in the RECORD, I include the following glossary of terms used to keep the wheels turning in Government and industry:

Program: Any assignment that cannot be completed with one phone call.
Channels: The trail left by interoffice memos.
Coordinator: The guy who has a desk between two expediters.
Consultant or expert: Any ordinary guy more than 50 miles away.
Under consideration: Never heard of it.
Under active consideration: We are looking in the files for it.

Conference: Where conversation is substituted for the dreariness of labor and the loneliness of thought.

Committee: A means for evading responsibility.

Board: First, made of wood; second, long and narrow; and, third, sometimes warped.

Reliable source: The guy you just met.

Informed source: The guy who just told the guy you just met.

Unimpeachable source: The guy who started the rumor originally.

Make a survey: Need more time to think of an answer.

Note and initial: Spread the responsibility.

Clarification: Fill in the background with so many details that the foreground goes underground.

Check the files: Ask the janitor to look through yesterday's sweepings.

Finalize: Scratch gravel to cover errors.

—*Rep. John Hinshaw (R-Calif.)*
February 23, 1956

I AM A SLOB

Mr. BAKER. Mr. President, I do not often indulge in personal observations, and I apologize to the Senate for doing so. In this morning's Washington Post, from page B3 under "Personalities," in the center column, the fourth paragraph, I wish to read what was printed.

President Reagan has been named as one of America's 10 best dressed men in the government category, barely beating Senate Majority Leader Howard Baker and former vice president Walter Mondale.

The poll, taken by the Tailor's Council of America, named John Travolta in the film category; Hal Linden, TV; Julius (Doctor J) Irving, athlete; Monty Hall, philanthropist; Don Rickles, comedian; Julio Iglesias, singer; and Jose Feliciano, musician, as winners of their categories.

I have had a lot of surprises in my life, Mr. President, but never as big as the surprise which faced me this morning before breakfast when reading the Washington Post. I want to say I have absolutely no taste in clothes, that I am so bad that my wife will not let me out of the house in the morning without first standing for inspection. I have even known in my lifetime tailors and haberdashers to call me on the telephone and urge that I must come and choose a suit or else they would send me one. During the Watergate hearings, I was flooded with gifts of clothing because people were ashamed to see me representing the forces of light and reason in my chosen attire. I am a slob. I am flattered in the extreme.

Mr. President, I began to wonder about the choice of the Tailor's Council of America. Then I noticed that they chose, in the category of motion picture films, John Travolta, who is almost always seen in a tee-shirt; they chose Hal Linden in television. Hal Linden has not had a haircut since early childhood.

Julius "Dr. J." Irving for the category of athletes, who is seldom seen by the American public except in his underwear.

So it goes. That did take a little of the luster, burnish, and polish away from this accolade.

With these remarks, I wish to thank the Tailor's Council of America for this award and recognition, but I must also tell them that, one of these days, we have to understand each other better.

Now, Mr. President, down to the matters at hand.

—*Sen. Howard H. Baker, Jr. (R-Tenn.)*
November 2, 1983

EVERY DAY'S A HOLIDAY

National Cheeseburger Week and its Commemorative Cousins

EVERY
DAY'S
A
HOLIDAY

WHOPPER WEEK

Mr. MAZZOLI. Mr. Speaker, today I am introducing a resolution proclaiming the week of October 7-13, 1984 as "National Cheeseburger Week" in honor of the 50th anniversary of the creation of the cheeseburger.

I have offered this resolution because the cheeseburger was "created" in October 1934 at Kaelin's Restaurant in my hometown of Louisville, KY. My family and I ate often at Kaelin's over the years and always cheeseburgers were the main fare.

Today cheeseburgers are as much a part of American tradition as baseball, hot dogs, and apple pie. Cheeseburgers go with families and picnics and barbeques. Cheeseburgers are a part of our daily vocabulary, and they provide a well-balanced and inexpensive meal in this era of eating on the run.

I hope my colleagues will join me in supporting this resolution.

—Rep. Romano L. Mazzoli (D-Ky.)
July 24, 1984

HELL, NO

Mr. SYMMS. I am happy to have the committee tied up with legislation like this, rather than tied up with unionizing Government employees; but

I was wondering, does the gentleman plan to have a Heaven Day, as well as an Earth Day?

Mr. LEHMAN. According to parliamentary procedure, we can only ask for an Earth Day this year and we are only requesting it this year alone.

Mr. SYMMS. There is only an Earth Day, no heavenly aspirations?

Mr. LEHMAN. I did not understand that.

Mr. SYMMS. There will be no Heaven Day? We are just going to have an Earth Day?

Mr. LEHMAN. We will all have our Heaven Day soon enough.

Mr. SYMMS. I would not bet on it.

Mr. LEHMAN. The gentleman can speak for himself.

Mr. SYMMS. I thank the gentleman for his compliment.

—*Reps. Steven D. Symms (R-Idaho) and William Lehman (D-Fla.)*
March 18, 1975

CONE HEAD—I

Mr. DE LA GARZA. Mr. Speaker, I have introduced a resolution declaring July Ice Cream Month and July 15 as Ice Cream Day.

I would invite my colleagues to join with me, if you have not already signed the resolution. Ice cream is good for you.

If you feel dejected or frustrated, eat ice cream; if the legislative processes frustrate you, eat ice cream; if you are happy and want to celebrate, eat ice cream. Not only will you help an industry and American workers but it is good, it is just plain good.

—*Rep. E de la Garza (D-Tex.)*
June 7,1984

CONE HEAD—II

Mr. D'AMATO. Mr. President, it is with great enthusiasm that I rise today to honor a fine and cherished tradition: ice cream. I, like members of 98 percent of all American households, appreciate a cone or dish of ice cream in the heat of July; therefore, it is most appropriate that July is National Ice Cream Month and that the second Sunday, yesterday, July 14, was National Ice Cream Day or Sundae Sunday.

—Sen. Alfonse M. D'Amato (R-N.Y.)
July 15, 1985

NUEVO MEXICO

Mr. DOMENICI. Mr. President, I shortly shall send to the desk for its immediate consideration, and I ask unanimous consent that it be in order to do so, a resolution that will recognize today, June 13, 1986 as "New Mexico Is a State Day." This resolution is necessary to draw attention to a reality that is frequently overlooked, either through ignorance or hearing impairment.

I ask my colleagues in the Senate to recognize that New Mexico is a state.

I ask that my colleagues recognize that I was not sent to Washington, along with my distinguished junior Senator, Senator JEFF BINGAMAN, from a foreign country but from a State of the Union. We were both elected by U.S. citizens who reside in the sovereign State of New Mexico. For those who are not familiar with the geographic location of my State, the Land of Enchantment, it is directly south of Colorado, east of Arizona, west of Texas, and north of the Mexican border. I repeat, north of the Mexican border. I repeat, north of the Mexican border. It was established as the 47th State in the Union in 1912.

Recently, a congressional candidate, David Cargo, a former Governor of my State, was informed by the Treasury Department that 30 percent of his Treasury bills would be withheld because he lived in a foreign country....

Mr. President, this is not the first time that New Mexico has suffered an identity crisis at the hands of the Federal Government. The State Department has been known to refer my staff to its foreign affairs desk. Grocery and drug stores in the District have refused to honor New Mexico drivers' licenses, stating that it is their store's policy to take checks only from American citizens. When individuals are planning vacations in my beautiful State, there are frequent inquiries concerning visas, immunization, and the relative drinkability of our water. There are 1.3 million people who reside in the beautiful and sovereign State of New Mexico, fifth largest State of the Union, by area. There are no horses that are tied to hitching posts on Main Street. In fact, we have removed most of the hitching posts from most of our cities. We use U.S. currency, not pesos....

In this resolution, which I am joined in by my good friend, Senator BINGAMAN, who is also from New Mexico, elected by American citizens, we have summarized all the things we are, all the things our State stands for, and some of the things we have contributed to our national well-being. We now send this resolution to the desk and ask for its immediate consideration....

Mr. RUDMAN addressed the chair.

The PRESIDING OFFICER. The Senator from New Mexico.

Mr. RUDMAN. I wonder if my friend from New Mexico would yield for a question.

Mr. DOMENICI. I would be pleased to yield to my good friend.

Mr. RUDMAN. I find it very hard to believe that the Department of the Treasury would have made such a grievous error, and I wonder whether or not the Senator from New Mexico might not be missing something.

As the chairman of the Budget Committee, is it possible that because of Gramm-Rudman we have eliminated New Mexico?

Mr. DOMENICI. Well, I plan to leave here in about 45 minutes to go up to the Senator's State. I thought I was going up there to pay him honor and homage. I guarantee I would not be going up there if Gramm-Rudman eliminated us as a State of the United States.

Mr. RUDMAN. Will my friend yield for just one last question? I wonder if my friends from New Mexico might have considered that there might be some advantages to allowing this situation to ripen. After all, if you were expelled from the Union, I expect the Senator from New Mexico would immediately ask for a large block of foreign aid money.

Mr. DOMENICI. Let me say to my good friend, the fate of foreign aid in the national budget is not better than any of the other expenditures. I do not think we would be any better off. But perhaps we will ask New Mexicans if they want to consider that alternative.

Mr. RUDMAN. There is always the other alternative of a foreign military sales agreement with this administration. I expect that the people of New Mexico might like Stinger missiles, Sidewinder missiles and even Harpoon missiles to defend the vast ocean spaces of the State of New Mexico.

Mr. DOMENICI. In fact, we do need it because the Rio Grande does run there. I would tell Senators, however, it does not have any water in it half of the year.

The PRESIDING OFFICER. Is there further debate on the resolution?...

Mr. BOSCHWITZ addressed the Chair....

Mr. BOSCHWITZ. Mr. President, I rise in opposition to this resolution. [Laughter.]

I am not all rhapsodic about the idea of allowing New Mexico to stay in the Union. Had I been here a little earlier, perhaps I would have opposed its inclusion in the first place.

Mr. DOMENICI. You mean the resolution or statehood?

Mr. BOSCHWITZ. Both. [Laughter.]

I might say that I, too, am identified as a close friend—indeed, as the Senator from Washington said, a close disciple—of the senior Senator from New Mexico. But that makes no difference.

I say to my friend from New Mexico that if we are successful in defeating this resolution and he moves on to other endeavors, I rise on the Budget Committee—I rise from fourth ranking to third. [Laughter.]

That certainly is a consideration that the Senate will want to consider as it looks at this motion.

Furthermore, there has been a degree of confusion. "DOMENICI from New Mexico"—that itself is almost a contradiction in terms. So that the Department of the Treasury and others are right to be confused.

Mr. DOMENICI. If they are confused about that—

Mr. BOSCHWITZ. I do not yield the floor, Mr. President. [Laughter.]

I might say that there is another consideration. My State of Minnesota borders up against Canada. We have often talked about seceding and joining our northern neighbor, and perhaps if New Mexico would lead the way, we would be emboldened to make this move.

Furthermore, constitutionally, as the Senator knows, I am the only Senator who is forbidden to be President of this country, because I was born abroad. In the event we seceded and created our own Nation of Minnesota, that restriction would be removed.

So when you came up with this resolution and you said that New Mexico, suddenly, should get this special consideration, I hastened to the floor in order to raise these objections.

I will not let this lie and will vote vigorously against this resolution.

I yield the floor.

Mr. DOMENICI. Mr. President, we are going to wait until he leaves, before we take the vote. [Laughter.]

I want to make one other comment: There is an objection to this, I understand, and I say to the distinguished acting majority leader that I hope he will help me out. Senator HATFIELD has objected to our considering this. I hope that you, in your capacity as leader, feel confident enough to let us go ahead with this, or you could see to it that that reservation is removed.

Mr. LONG. Mr. President, will the Senator yield?

Mr. DOMENICI. I yield.

Mr. LONG. Mr. President, if we are going to permit New Mexico to remain in the Union, it seems to me we ought to take a little more time and see if we can have a more imaginative name. Arizona got a name of its own. I do not know what the derivation of it was. Colorado is a beautiful name and is something imaginative. I do not know where Texas came from.

Talking about a minimum of imagination, when one from Mexico separates it from Mexico and says, "We'll call this New Mexico," that does not seem imaginative to me.

Mr. DOMENICI. You think of a new one for us, and we will think of a new one for you.

Mr. LONG. Maybe you can think of a new one for New Orleans.

In any event, it seems to me that between now and the time we pass this resolution, or before it is printed, the Senator might at least put his mind to see if he can think of a more imaginative name.

Mr. DOMENICI. I hope we will pass this resolution in about 30 seconds, and I do not have a very good imagination. So I hope you will not hold me to it.

Mr. SIMPSON. Mr. President, when the majority leader asked if I would drop by the Chamber and check on things, I never dreamed I would have to come by just as we were dabbling in this activity. It is very fascinating, I might add—more than I could have ever dreamed of in the way of a resolution.

It is Friday the 13th. A little levity is called for as we grapple with the tax reform issue. Good humor is something I have learned to enjoy from my friend the Senator from New Mexico, a spirited man. When he came on Earth, they called him "Bocci," which has a name in Italy—a red-headed bocci ball. He is one of the most extraordinary of our colleagues.

I see the Senator from Minnesota lurking nearby. He does know his numbers. He referred to the fact that he would be No. 3 if Senator DOME-NICI were removed from the scene. He keeps track of those things. He refers to me as No. 57 and refers to himself continually as No. 56, which is more offensive. [Laughter.]

Mr. BOSCHWITZ. Mr. President, will the Senator yield?

Mr. SIMPSON. I yield.

Mr. BOSCHWITZ. If we could get rid of him, I would be 55 and you would be 56. [Laughter.]

Mr. SIMPSON. I am ready for that. [Laughter.] There are really two of us in this body who will never be President of the United States, and they are the Senator from Minnesota, who was born in Germany, and me. I have three electoral votes. [Laughter.]

So New Mexico is a State, so far as I am concerned. A great one. If Senator PACKWOOD is ready to go forward with his labors, if someone has an amendment by now, we can go forward.

So I say to New Mexico, a land where the canary bird sings bass, you are a State; I pronounce you so; and, in the words of the Wizard of Oz, it shall be so. [Laughter.]

Mr. DOMENICI. I thank the Senator. I will do the same for Wyoming some day.

Mr. LONG. Mr. President, word has reached the minority leader, Mr. BYRD, that this resolution is being considered, and he has sent word to me that I may state for the RECORD that he, too, on behalf of the Democratic side of the aisle, is willing to agree that New Mexico should be permitted to remain a part of this Union. I want the RECORD to show that. There is no objection on this side of the aisle.

Mr. DOMENICI. I ask whether Senator BINGAMAN wants to thank his distinguished minority leader, Senator BYRD, who is not here but sends his best wishes to us.

Mr. BINGAMAN. I thank him. And I recommend to my senior colleague that he not ask for a rollcall vote.

Mr. DOMENICI. I want to finish this. I do not know what is going to happen.

I do know one thing for certain: Senator BOSCHWITZ will not move up in seniority on the Budget Committee under any circumstance, I assure him, whether we are in the Union or out. We have arranged for that. [Laughter.]

I thought he was going to come here and be nice. It is often very difficult for him to do that, but I thought on this one occasion he would be other than his usual self.

We hope that you would succeed in seceding, because then people like SLADE GORTON would move up in seniority on the Budget Committee, and that would be helpful.

Mr. President, I ask unanimous consent that it be in order to consider the resolution I have sent to the desk on behalf of myself and my distinguished junior colleague, Senator BINGAMAN.

The PRESIDING OFFICER. Without objection, it is so ordered.

Is there further debate on the resolution?

Without objection, the resolution is agreed to, and the preamble is agreed to.

Mr. BOSCHWITZ. I would like to have at least a voice vote on that, Mr. President, if we could have a voice vote on that.

Mr. DOMENICI. Although the Senator has no right to that after the vote was announced, he can get a rollcall vote. One of these days he will learn the rules. And I have no objection.

The PRESIDING OFFICER. If the Senator will address the Chair, all Senators in favor of the resolution say, "Aye." All opposed, "No."

Mr. BOSCHWITZ. No.

The PRESIDING OFFICER. The "ayes" appear to have it. The "ayes" have it.

—*Sens. Pete V. Domenici (R-N. Mex.), Warren Rudman (R-N.H.), Rudy Boschwitz (R-Minn.), Russell B. Long (D-La.), and Alan K. Simpson (R-Wyo.)*
June 13, 1986

CARPET BRAGGERS

Mr. D'AMATO. Mr. President, I rise today to join my distinguished colleague from Georgia in cosponsoring a joint resolution designating the week of April 18, 1986, through April 27, 1986, as "National Carpet and Floorcovering Week."

Carpet and floorcovering manufacturers have been an important part of the American business community since the first carpet mill was established in 1791. Today, carpet manufacturers are located in 23 States including my State of New York....

—Sen. Alfonse M. D'Amato (R-N.Y.)
April 9, 1986

ONLY A JOKE

Mr. RONCALIO. Mr. Speaker, I take the well of the House to congratulate the American energy companies who have announced this morning they will reject Government guarantees and Government grants in proceeding with a program for synthetic fuels. I am particularly grateful to our oil and other energy companies when they admit they do not need Government assistance in their work.

Also I commend the American Banking Association for admitting that they could use reform, and in their approval of the bill now in the committee chaired by the gentleman from Wisconsin (Mr. REUSS).

Also I commend the AFL-CIO labor leadership for the nonstrike agreement, and I laud American management for agreeing to give labor two or three seats on the boards of directors of all American corporations.

And a happy April 1 to you, Mr. Speaker.

—Rep. Teno Roncalio (D-Wyo.)
April 1, 1976

IT'S A HOOT

Mr. BAKER. Mr. President, I would like to offer a hearty sa-a-lute on the 15th anniversary of television's most successful syndicated show, "Hee-Haw."...

—Sen. Howard H. Baker, Jr. (R-Tenn.)
June 14, 1983

NO MICKEY MOUSE OPERATION

H.J. RES. 122
To designate the week beginning July 13, 1987, as "Snow White Week".

IN THE HOUSE OF REPRESENTATIVES
January 29, 1987

Mr. MOORHEAD (for himself, Mr. BERMAN, Mr. DORNAN of California, Mr. WAXMAN, Mr. DANNEMEYER, and Mr. DREIER) introduced the following joint resolution; which was referred to the Committee on Post Office and Civil Service

JOINT RESOLUTION

To designate the week beginning July 13, 1987, as "Snow White Week".

Whereas Walt Disney released his classic film "Snow White and the Seven Dwarfs" fifty years ago, on December 21, 1937;

Whereas "Snow White and the Seven Dwarfs" marked a milestone in motion picture history as the first full-length animated feature film;

Whereas the art of animation reached exciting new heights with "Snow White and the Seven Dwarfs";

Whereas for the more than 750 artists who worked on the film "Snow White and the Seven Dwarfs" was a labor of love;

Whereas the movie soundtrack album for "Snow White and the Seven Dwarfs" was the first original soundtrack recording ever released;

Whereas "Snow White and the Seven Dwarfs" set a new standard for the integration of musical numbers with action scenes in a movie musical;

Whereas "Snow White and the Seven Dwarfs" was cited for a special Academy Award as "a significant screen innovation which has charmed millions and pioneered a great new entertainment field for the motion picture cartoon"; and

Whereas "Snow White and the Seven Dwarfs" has delighted the hearts of people of all ages throughout the world for the past fifty years: Now, therefore, be it

Resolved by the Senate and House of Representatives of the United States of America in Congress assembled, That the week beginning

July 13, 1987, is designated as "Snow White Week", and the President is authorized and requested to issue a proclamation calling upon the people of the United States to celebrate the week with appropriate ceremonies and activities.

—*Reps. Carlos J. Moorhead (R-Calif.), Howard L. Berman (D-Calif.), Robert K. Dornan (R-Calif.) Henry A. Waxman (D-Calif.), William E. Dannemeyer (R-Calif.), and David Dreier (R-Calif.)*
January 29, 1987

STALK IS CHEAP

H.J. RES. 137
Designating the month of May as "National Asparagus Month".

IN THE HOUSE OF REPRESENTATIVES
February 4, 1987

Mr. SHUMWAY (for himself, Mr. COELHO, Mr. PASHAYAN, Mr. LEHMAN of California, Mr. SCHUETTE, Mr. HERGER, Mr. PANETTA, and Mr. MORRISON of Washington) introduced the following joint resolution; which was referred to the Committee on Post Office and Civil Service

JOINT RESOLUTION

Designating the month of May as "National Asparagus Month".

Whereas the genus asparagus, a member of the lily family, originated along the shores of the Mediterranean Sea and on its many islands;
Whereas asparagus was considered a culinary delicacy and used for medicinal purposes by the ancient Greeks and Romans;
Whereas asparagus has been grown in America since the 1600's for its nutritional and decorative value in floral arrangements;
Whereas two hundred and twenty-three million pounds of asparagus was grown in the United States comprising a total value of approximately $137,000,000 in 1986; and
Whereas the delectable vegetable is low in calories and fat, and contains large amounts of calcium and phosphorus as well as vitamins A, C, and

B, all important components of a well balanced diet: Now, therefore, be it

Resolved by the Senate and House of Representatives of the United States of America in Congress assembled, That the month of May is designated as "National Asparagus Month". The President is requested to issue a proclamation calling upon the people of the United States to observe such month with appropriate ceremonies and activities.

—Reps. Norman D. Shumway (R-Calif.), Tony Coelho (D-Calif.) Charles Pashay-an, Jr. (R-Calif.), Richard H. Lehman (D-Calif.) Bill Schuette (R-Mich.), Wally Herger (R-Calif.), Leon E. Panetta (D-Calif.), and Sid Morrison (R-Wash.)
February 4, 1987

YOU COULD LOOK IT UP

Mr. GREEN. Mr. Speaker, as Representative of the district housing Simon & Schuster, Inc., publisher of America's most honored dictionary, I should like to take a moment of this chamber's time to recognize the importance of lexicography on this, National Dictionary Day.

As noted in Webster's New World Dictionary 2d College Edition, "Americanism" is defined as "A word, phrase, or usage originating in, or peculiar to, American English." I would like to share a number of these with my esteemed colleagues: Champ, geek, hoagie, gizmo, scuba, snafu, beeline, thinktank, clipboard, movie, cloudburst, stevedore, sidewalk, freightcar, French toast, Canadian bacon, Chinatown, English muffin, chow mein, chicken a la king, caramba, cloverleaf, coffee table, preempt, paycheck, riproaring, ripsnorting, shovelhead, teddy bear, internal revenue, sideburns, belly flop, letterman, jigsaw, bathtub, barbeque, jumbo, babysitter, chili, lacrosse, teepee, roughneck, floozy, Mickey Mouse, smog, catnap, coyote, crackerjack, and of course, caucus.

Thanks to David Guralnick, editor-in-chief of Webster's New World Dictionary for supplying us with 14,000 Americanisms, in addition to the small sample listed above.

—Rep. Bill Green (R-N.Y.)
October 16, 1985

MR. SPEAKER, I HAVE TWO MORE JOKES

It Reminds Me of the Story . . .

MR. SPEAKER,
I HAVE
TWO MORE
JOKES

ON THE RIGHT TRACK

Mr. CHILES. I say to the Senator from New York that in 9 hours and whatever minutes it will be, there will be the shootout at the OK Corral. By that time, whether the golden egg has been found or not, Gary Cooper will walk down the street and we will have the guns begin to go off. It seems to me we should be having some kind of dialog, we should be trying to determine how we put this package together.

I am reminded of a story of the young man who applied for employment with a railroad company, and he was going to be a tower operator, an operator in the control tower of the train yard. They were showing him the equipment. He seemed to be able to grasp all of this.

They said, "Now, we want to give you a little test."

They said, "The express is coming in down the east track and it is going to arrive at 2:15. The local is coming in down the west track and it is to cross at 2:15, but someone has opened a switch. It is now on the main track. What would you do?

He said, "I would go get my brother."

"Why in the world would you do that?"

He said, "He ain't never seen a train wreck, either."

It seems to me, Mr. President, that now should be the time, before we send for our brother, that we ought to do something to avoid this train wreck. We know the trains are coming down this track and will collide. Yet we are just allowing the time to go and go while one side continues to search for the golden egg.

Mr. MOYNIHAN. I wonder if I may have permission, in the circumstances—it is a beautiful day outside and nothing is taking place inside. The west front of the Capitol is falling down. At least we could watch that while we wait for the time to run out. May I be excused?

Mr. CHILES. I would be happy to excuse the distinguished Senator from New York.

Mr. MOYNIHAN. I thank my distinguished friend and colleague and leave.

> — *Sens. Lawton Chiles (D-Fla.) and Daniel Patrick Moynihan (D-N.Y.)*
> *May 11, 1983*

A SLOW DAY

Mr. LEE. Mr. President, I am not responsible for the seats in the Senate Chamber not being filled. I am reminded of the preacher, who, after preaching a while, said to one of the ushers, "Wake Brother Brown up." The usher replied, "Wake him up yourself; you put him to sleep." [Laughter.]

> — *Sen. Josh Lee (D-Okla.)*
> *June 23, 1939*

GOLDEN OLDIE

Mr. MATSUNAGA. I am reminded of the time when Emanuel Celler was in the House, and I served with him. Emanuel Celler was the oldest Member of that body at that time. He was in the well, speaking in support of a measure I had introduced, and he forgot certain facts about which I reminded him.

He said, "Oh yes, yes. How clearly I recall that now. You know, there are three signs of aging. The first is that you tend to forget things rather easily—and for the life of me, I don't know what the other two things are." [Laughter.]

> — *Sen. Spark M. Matsunaga (D-Hawaii)*
> *March 12, 1980*

S.O.S.

Mr. SCOTT. This kind of amendment reminds me of an anecdote told me in another context by the distinguished Senator from New Hampshire (Mr. McINTYRE) recently, and that is that these amendments, increasingly, indicate that there may be a certain lack of logical persuasiveness. The story is about two inexperienced hunters who went into the woods after game. The game warden readily identified them as being tyros at the sport and warned them that they might get lost.

He said, "If you do get lost, the signal for distress is to fire three shots in rapid succession."

In due course, they did get lost.

One of them said to the other, "You had better fire three shots."

So he fired three shots. Nothing happened.

After waiting for about an hour or two, the first hunter said, "You had better fire another three shots."

So the second hunter fired a second round of three shots. They waited another hour or so, and still nothing happened.

Again, the first hunter turned to the second and said, in great distress, "I guess you had better fire three more shots."

His friend said, "I can't. I have run out of arrows."

—Sen. Hugh Scott (R-Pa.)
March 6, 1970

GOOD NEWS, BAD NEWS

Mr. UDALL. Mr. Chairman, as I rise here I am reminded of the worn-out story of the man who was asked how he felt when he saw his mother-in-law drive his brand new uninsured Cadillac off the cliff. He answered that he had mixed emotions.

—Rep. Morris K. Udall (D-Ariz.)
May 29, 1963

DOUBLE INDEMNITY

Mr. ERVIN. I ask the Senator if he does not agree with me that those of our brethren who wish to put upon us, in addition to our State registrars not only the voting referee but also the Federal enrollment officer, are like the fellow who had what he considered to be a cantankerous mother-in-law, and who received a telegram from the undertaker saying, "Your mother-in-law died today. Shall we cremate or bury?"

I ask the Senator whether this chap was not like our friends who wish to add to the voting referee provision the enrollment provision, when he wired back to the undertaker, "Your telegram received. Take no chances. Cremate and bury."

—Sen. Sam J. Ervin, Jr. (D-N.C.)
April 4, 1960

FAST COMPANY

Mr. JACOBS. Mr. Speaker, will the gentleman yield?

Mr. VISCLOSKY. I yield to the gentleman from Indiana.

Mr. JACOBS. I thank the gentleman for yielding and for taking this occasion to honor our dear colleague, Ray Madden, who, as anybody can plainly see, is utterly indestructible. He will live forever. He already has a good start on that.

There are about 10,000 Ray Madden stories, but I think the one I will enter into the RECORD right now is the one about the year the time-zone legislation came before the Committee on Rules, and Bill Colmer of Mississippi was chairing and Ray Madden was a member of the committee. Bill was usually strictly business, and I am not sure how happy he was about this, but Ray, when he had his turn to ask questions, said that out in Indianapolis, Indiana, a man walked into the bus station and asked the ticket salesman, "When does the bus leave for Lebanon, Indiana?"

The ticket salesman said, "Ten o'clock."

He said, "What time does it get there?"

The ticket salesman said, "Ten o'clock."

The man turned around, walked away, and came back and said, "What time did you say that bus leaves?"

The ticket salesman said, "Ten o'clock."

"What time does it get there?"

"Ten o'clock."

He walked away again, and the ticket salesman said, "Say, do you want to buy a ticket for Lebanon?" And the gentleman said, "No, I don't, but would you mind if I stayed around and watched that bus take off?"

— Reps. Andrew Jacobs, Jr. (D-Ind.) and Peter J. Visclosky (D-Ind.)
February 25, 1986

HEAVEN CAN WAIT

Mr. SIMPSON. I guess I often think of the great phrase when President Grant sent one of his loyal members of the Cabinet off to the West. He said, "Write me back and tell me what it is they need out there."

The general wired back and said, "All this place needs is good people and water." Grant wired back and said, "That is all hell needs."

(Laughter.)

— Sen. Alan K. Simpson (R-Wyo.)
January 26, 1984

A RELIGIOUS EXPERIENCE

Mr. HAYS. The story was about this Baptist Deacon, and you know how we Baptists feel about horse racing. He sneaked off with all the money he could spare to the racetrack. He didn't know very much about the horses, but he looked around, and there was a Catholic priest standing by a horse. He thought, well, that horse must be all right. It was number 17.

So he put all of his money on number 17 because of the priest, and he just knew that horse had to be all right.

The horse came in last. The Baptist went over to the Catholic priest, and he said, "Say, you caused me to lose every dollar I brought out here."

The priest said, "Why are you blaming me for your bad betting practices?"

He said, "I saw you give number 17 your blessing."

The priest said, "That is just the trouble with you Baptists. You don't know the difference between a blessing and the last rites."

— Rep. Brooks Hays (D-Ark.)
May 19, 1977

HANG IT ALL

Mr. MENGES. Gentlemen, I think I told this story when I appeared before the Interstate Commerce Committee, with regard to this bill, about the Irishman who was about to be hanged. The sheriff asked him whether he would like to inspect the gallows, and he said he would not mind. After Mike was done inspecting the sheriff asked him whether he had anything to say, and he said he thought the damn thing was not safe. [Laughter.]

— Rep. Franklin Menges (R-Pa.)
June 15, 1926

OPEN AND SHUT CASE

MR. SWINDALL. I thank the Chairman.

Mr. Chairman, I can still remember some 19 months ago after being sworn in to this august body the President of the United States inviting each of the freshman Members and their spouse to the White House for a get-acquainted dinner.

At that dinner he shared an anecdote about a freshman Member of Congress who went over to Georgetown with a Member of the Senate and a member of the administration to discuss, undoubtedly, a piece of legislation, that kept them in Georgetown until the wee hours of the morning.

They came out to the Congressman's car, only to have the Congressman discover that he had locked his keys in the car. At that point he turned to his two colleagues and told them he was going back into the restaurant to get a coat hanger so he could pry the lock open. At that point the gentleman from the Senate said he really did not think that that was a good idea. He was afraid somebody would misunderstand what he was doing and that before they could explain themselves they would find headlines the next morning saying that they had been caught in Georgetown breaking into a car.

Well, at that point the Congressman said he agreed, and what would the Senator suggest. The Senator said, "Well, I think I have a pocket knife that I think I can cut just enough of the rubber so that I can slip my finger in and unlock the door." Well, at that point the Congressman shook his head and said, "I don't think that's a very good idea either. I am afraid somebody will see what you are doing and think that you are just too stupid to know how to use a coat hanger."

Well, at that point the fellow from the State Department who had been watching all of this transpire looked at both of them and said, "Frankly, I don't care how you resolve it, I just hope you do it in a hurry because it is getting ready to rain and, frankly, I am afraid you are not going to get into it in time to put your top up."

— Rep. Pat Swindall (R-Ga.)
July 29, 1986

OH, GOD

Mr. HAYS. Then I recall something that involved my good Baptist friend, Bill D. Moyers....

President Johnson called on Bill one day to open a Cabinet meeting with prayer. Bill was sitting at the end of the Cabinet table, and when he had finished the prayer, the President said, "Bill, we couldn't hear you up here."

Bill said, "I wasn't talking to you, Mr. President."

— Rep. Brooks Hays (D-Ark.)
May 19, 1977

MAN OF THE HOUSE

Mr. JACOBS. There is a story about a man who shows his friend through his new house. "This is the living room, here is the dining room. This is the Florida room," he says, "and that is my wife" and there she is sitting on the love seat just kissing up a storm with another man. And they go on into the kitchen and sit down and the host pours his guest a cup of coffee and then he pours himself a cup of coffee. And the guest cannot stand it any longer and he says, "What about the guy in the Florida room?" And the host says, "Let him get his own coffee."

— Rep. Andrew Jacobs, Jr. (D-Ind.)
June 27, 1984

FLAME AND FORTUNE

Mr. WILLIAMS. Two old drunkards were in the habit of coming to Lebanon, Kentucky, twice a week to get drunk together. They would buy a two-gallon jug of whiskey and get out in some old house and lie around until the last drop was gone. They kept this up for awhile, but in the course of the years one of them died. His old friend came in on Saturday and inquired about him. The boys told him, "He is dead; have you not heard of it?" "Oh, no. What killed him?" "Well, you know he has been drinking hard for a good many years, and the doctors say that the whiskey was taken into his circulation, and so saturated his breath and his blood that one night the old man before going to bed went to blow out the candle, and his breath caught on fire and he was burned to death." "Gracious heavens!" said the surviving friend. "What a horrible death! Boys, send for a preacher, give me a Bible, and bring me in a magistrate, and let me take the oath quick." This request was complied with. The old man took hold of the holy volume, kissed it, lifted his hand and his eyes, and began: "I swear before Almighty God and these witnesses that I will never, during life, blow out another candle."

— Sen. John S. Williams (D-Miss.)
1902

INDENTURED

Mr. UDALL. I remember another story about the minister making a hellfire-and-damnation speech saying: "Brothers and sisters, judgment day is coming. You are all going to have to meet your Maker on that terrible judgment day. There is going to be lightning and thunder, there are going to be earthquakes, and there is going to be weeping and wailing and, brothers and sisters, you are all going to gnash your teeth." And then a little lady in the front row said: "Brother, I ain't got no teeth." The minister said: "On that terrible day, believe me, madam, teeth will be provided."

— Rep. Morris K. Udall (D-Ariz.)
June 29, 1977

OUT OF SIGHT, OUT OF MIND

The SPEAKER. Brooks was such a great man and such a beautiful story-teller. I remember well the last occasion I had to meet with him.
He said, "I understand you have become an avid golf fan."
I said, "I am."
He said, "Did you hear the story about the 85-year-old fellow who went out to be a caddy? The golf pro looked at him and he said, 'Well, you are too old to carry the bag, but you can walk as a forecaddy. Are your eyes good?'
"The old man said, 'My eyes are perfect.'
"So he went out and a fellow hit the ball about 270 yards.
"'Did you see where it went?' he asked.
"'I sure did. My eyes are perfect,' the old man replied.
"'Where did it go?' he asked.
"And the old man said, 'I forget.'"

— Rep. Thomas P. (Tip) O'Neill, Jr. (D-Mass.)
May 17, 1982

GIVE OR TAKE AN INCH

Mr. DIRKSEN. I think sometimes of the fellow who saw an automobile accident out home when he was put on the stand to testify. Counsel said, "Did you see the accident?" He said, "Yes, sir." Counsel asked, "How far away were you when the accident happened?" Witness said, "Twenty-two feet, nine and three-quarter inches." Counsel looked at the court and looked at the jury and said, "Well, Smartie, tell the court and jury how do you know it was twenty-two feet, nine and three-quarter inches." Witness replied, "When it happened I took out a tape measure and measured from where I stood to the point of impact, because I knew some darned lawyer was going to ask me that question."

— Sen. Everett M. Dirksen (R-Ill.)
1959

DRAIN BRAIN

Mr. NUNN. Will Rogers once said that the way to end World War I, I believe, was to drain the Atlantic Ocean and there would not be any German submarines. Somebody asked him how he was going to do it. He said:

"Well, that is a detail. I am not a detail man."

— Sen. Sam Nunn (D-Ga.)
June 3, 1975

MIDDLE OF THE ROAD

Mr. ROBERTSON. I would rather put it this way. Once upon an occasion a stranger was traveling in Scotland, and he said to the Scotsman, "Is this the road to Edinburgh?"

The Scotsman said, "Yes, my friend, but you will have to turn around."

—Sen. A. Willis Robertson (D-Va.)
April 4, 1960

FOUR BITS

Mr. ERVIN. If I may tell a story as a basis for a question, down in North Carolina there was a fellow named George. George said to his friend Bill, "My wife is the most extravagant woman. She always wants 50 cents for this, 50 cents for that, and 50 cents for the other thing."

Bill said, "What does she do with all that money?"

George said, "She don't get it."

—Sen. Sam J. Ervin, Jr. (D-N.C.)
January 25, 1963

A SECOND OPINION

Mr. CHILES. It reminds me of the story about the fellow who fell off a cliff. As he was falling, he stuck out his hand, and he finally was able to grasp a branch. It was shaking, and dirt was falling off the roots, and he did not know whether the branch was going to hold him.

He cried out: "Help! Help!" There was no reply. He said: "Is anybody up there?"

Finally, a voice said: "I am here."

He said, "Who is there?"

The voice said, "It is I, the Lord. Have faith."

The fellow said: "I have faith."

The voice said: "Turn loose."

The fellow said: "Is anybody else up there?" [Laughter.]

—Sen. Lawton Chiles (D-Fla.)
May 3, 1984

BUT SERIOUSLY, FOLKS

Mr. HAYS. This is a story about the time I heard a lawyer speaking to his client, a widow. He said, "Did you hear your husband's last words?"

She said, "Sure."

He said, "What were they?"

She said, "'Go ahead and shoot. You couldn't hit the side of a barn.'"

I have never told you about a lad who was in the Arkansas penitentiary. His little wife wanted to hold the family together. They had a little hillside farm. She wrote to him and said, "When shall I plant the potatoes?"

He wrote back, "For goodness sake, don't dig around that garden bed. That's where my guns are buried."

The sheriff and his deputies intercepted the letter and rushed out there and dug up every square yard of that garden.

Then he wrote to his wife, "Now it's time to plant the potatoes."

—Rep. Brooks Hays (D-Ark.)
May 21, 1974

PIN THE TALE ON THE DONKEY

Mr. UDALL. Remember the old story about the old man who had his grandson on a donkey and they passed some people, and the people said: "Look at that little kid riding while his elderly grandfather has to walk." So the kid got off and the grandfather got on the donkey and they went along a little further and saw some other people who complained about the grandfather riding while the little kid was walking. So they said: "Why don't you both get on?" So they did, and they both rode on and came to another group of people who said: "Isn't it terrible that the poor little donkey is being loaded down with both of those people." So they got off and tied the donkey on a pole and carried him. They came to a bridge over a river, slipped, and they all fell off the bridge and drowned in the river. The moral of the story is: If you try to please everybody you are going to lose your donkey.

— Rep. Morris K. Udall (D-Ariz.)
June 29, 1977

CHALK TALK

Mr. HOLLINGS. It reminds me of a psychiatric test they gave a fellow when he walks into the doctor's office for his appointment.

The psychiatrist put a check mark on the blackboard. He said, "What do you think of that?"

He said, "That makes me think of sex."

The doctor drew a circle on the blackboard, and he said, "What do you think of when you see that?"

He said, "Sex."

Then the psychiatrist did a cross mark, and he said, "What do you think of that?"

He said, "That makes me think of sex."

The psychiatrist said, "Well, you are depraved, you are oversexed."

He said, "Me depraved?" He said, "You are the one drawing the dirty pictures."

—Sen. Ernest F. Hollings (D-S.C.)
September 10, 1975

NOT-SO-GREAT DEBATES

The Mystery
of the Misplaced Dot
and
Other Elementary Issues

NOT-SO-GREAT
DEBATES

A QUESTION OF SEMANTICS

Mr. ROBERT C. BYRD. Mr. President, does any Senator wish recognition before the motion to recess is made?

If not, I thank all Senators, and with best wishes for a good weekend and with the prospects for hard days and diligent labors and many tests in the immediate days ahead, weeks ahead, may I say to the distinguished Senator from California (Mr. HAYAKAWA) I hope that the Senate can adjourn sine die—is that the correct pronunciation, sine die?

Mr. HAYAKAWA. Absolutely, that is perfectly acceptable.

Mr. ROBERT C. BYRD. Well, if it is acceptable to the Senator from California, it must be all right. It would be acceptable to Webster, would it not?

Mr. HAYAKAWA. Fine.

Mr. ROBERT C. BYRD. Sine die.

By the way, I often hear and use the words "p-e-r s-e."

Mr. HAYAKAWA. Per se.

Mr. ROBERT C. BYRD. Pronounced per se as in bee, or per se, as in bay. I pronounce it both per se, and per se, I suppose either is correct—is either correct?

Mr. HAYAKAWA. I would prefer per se.

Mr. ROBERT C. BYRD. Per se.

I will stick with per se.

Mr. HAYAKAWA. Chacun à son gût.

Mr. ROBERT C. BYRD. Speaking of words, I have heard these words pronounced in a myriad of ways. Amicus curiae, amicus curiae.

How would the Senator from California pronounce those words? I have heard amicus curiae, amicus curiae, amicus curiae, amicus curiae, and amicus curiae?

Mr. HAYAKAWA. Amicus curiae.

Mr. ROBERT C. BYRD. The Senator would.

Mr. HAYAKAWA. Yes. I took 4 or 5 years of Latin. I never got over it.

Mr. ROBERT C. BYRD. Well, I am not one to argue with the Senator, but I think I will just continue amicus curiae.

Mr. HAYAKAWA. That is dreadful.

Mr. ROBERT C. BYRD. Let me see if I can think of another word.

Well, sufficient unto the day is the evil thereof.

—*Sens. Robert C. Byrd (D-W. Va.) and S.I. Hayakawa (R-Calif.)*
September 8, 1978

DOT'S ENTERTAINMENT

Mr. LOTT. Mr. Speaker, I yield myself such time as I may consume.

Mr. Speaker, the resolution I have offered raises a serious question regarding the integrity of House proceedings, for it goes to the very heart, the RECORD, of those proceedings....

As my colleagues know, since 1978, the Congress has been operating under a rule promulgated by the Joint Committee on Printing that requires that "statements or insertions in the RECORD where no part of them was spoken will be preceded and followed by a 'bullet' symbol," in order "to contribute to the historical accuracy of the RECORD." This still permits a Member to utter just one sentence of his speech, and it will appear in the RECORD without a bullet, as if he delivered it all....

Mr. Speaker, I do not know whether the case of the missing bullets is a crime of commission or omission. It is curious, though, that the Republican in the middle got a bullet to the head and tail-end of his remarks, while the two flanking Democrats weren't even grazed....

Mr. FRANK. Mr. Speaker, I was just having lunch, and when I overheard that the subject of dots had become a matter of congressional debate, I could not resist joining in, because I have not had a chance to debate dots for some time. We used to connect them, and now we are disconnecting them, I think, taking up the floor of the House time, but that is OK, because Members are free to do whatever they wish.

I did want to respond, as I understood what the majority whip was saying was that he was agreeing with what the minority leader was saying, although the minority leader seemed to be thinking they were in disagreement. That is, the majority whip was saying that the Committee on House Administration was the appropriate place for the great dot inquiry, because it was not a question of a rule, but whether or not there had been a mistake.

The minority leader was suggesting that we are responsible for administrative mistakes. The gentleman from Washington was saying that this very grave matter of the misplaced dot ought to be taken up in the administrative oversight committee, the Committee on House Administration.

So the gentleman from Washington was not suggesting that this matter should not be looked into. He was suggesting that the appropriate place to look into it is there; he was not in any way disclaiming that.

I did want to rise though, because the gentleman from Illinois did refer to an unfortunate situation where there were some apparent, deliberate altering of the remarks of the gentleman from Pennsylvania, and those of us who have been privileged to hear the remarks of the gentleman from Pennsylvania certainly do not want to have them altered; we prefer to have them preserved in pristine form.

I would want to make it clear that I hope no one is suggesting in this case that there was hanky-panky with the dots. That is, I hope that no one is suggesting that, unlike the previous case, there was some one deep in the bowels of the House who is dotting unfairly.

I think the American public has the right to be reassured that no one is playing fast and loose with the dots deliberately, and it was just an administrative error.

Mr. LOTT. Will the gentleman yield?

Mr. FRANK. I yield to the gentleman from Mississippi.

Mr. LOTT. Just for a couple of brief questions.

First of all, the gentleman is aware that these are generally referred to as bullets as opposed to dots, and—

Mr. FRANK. I will take back my time for 1 second. I understand the gentleman would rather call them bullets, and that is what the technical term is, but I thought it was useful that everybody should understand that the bullets we are talking about are in fact dots.

Mr. PASHAYAN. If the gentleman would yield, maybe we should compromise and call them BB's.

Mr. LOTT. Let me ask the gentleman this: Knowing the gentleman's interest in the way debate is handled here, and what the RECORD reflects, I would think that the gentleman would like for the record to reflect accurately what it said on the floor of the House, in that if it is not said it should not be so indicated; if it is spoken, it should be so indicated.

Also, that you would probably like to have a little bit stricter rule about making sure that we have an accurate record of the House.

Mr. FRANK. I would say to the gentleman, I very much agree. I also believe, I must say, in accuracy in reporting, and I think that while the technical jargon term is "bullet," we ought to be clear what we are talking about; it is a little black spot in the RECORD.

Yes; I am for accuracy. In fact, I do not ask that my remarks be revised and extended. Frankly, having said them, I think I have done my bit and I should not have to read them again, to go over them; that is for other people to do if they choose to.

The SPEAKER pro tempore. The time of the gentleman has expired.

Mr. FRANK. I ask for 1 additional minute.

Mr. FOLEY. I yield 2 additional minutes to the gentleman from Massachusetts.

Mr. FRANK. I thank the gentleman from Washington, who is the first person who has ever given me more than I have asked.

The point that I would make though, is that I believe that the RECORD ought to be accurate, but I think we have two separate issues here. One is, and the gentleman from Illinois is the one who underlined it: He said, look, we have a problem here, because someone has perhaps put a dot where—it is not that someone put a dot where they shouldn't have, but someone didn't put a dot where they should've.

The question of the missing dot was raised in a resolution—the gentleman from Washington says, let's find out. Because we do want the RECORD to be accurate as to what was said, and apparently we want the RECORD to be accurate as to what wasn't said....

— Reps. Trent Lott (R-Miss.), Barney Frank (D-Mass.) and
Charles Pashayan, Jr. (R-Calif.)
May 8, 1985

WHATEVER THE CASE MAY BE

Mr. SAM B. HALL, JR. Now, if a young child that is a patient of this doctor who has not signed the medicare assignment breaks an arm and is admitted to the emergency room of the hospital where he has not signed that form, will that doctor be allowed to go to that hospital and set the arm of the child?

Mr. JACOBS. It all depends.

Mr. SAM B. HALL, JR. On what?

Mr. JACOBS. Well, it is like having a date with Siamese twins and being asked if you had a good time and saying, "Well, yes and no."

It depends on whether the hospital continues its medicare relationship. The hospital itself could lose its medicare relationship and the doctor could practice there.

Mr. SAM B. HALL, JR. Well, I am not sure that the Siamese cat thing has anything to do with my question.

Mr. JACOBS. I did not say anything about a cat or a house. I said Siamese twins.

Mr. SAM B. HALL, JR. Twins. Well, twins or cats, whatever the case may be.

—Reps. Sam B. Hall, Jr. (D-Tex.) and Andrew Jacobs, Jr. (D-Ind.)
April 12, 1984

HATS OFF

Mr. SOLARZ. Mr. Chairman, I offer an amendment.

The Clerk read as follows:

Amendment offered by Mr. SOLARZ: At the end of title V (page 61, after line 13) add the following new section:

WEARING OF UNOBTRUSIVE RELIGIOUS HEADGEAR

SEC. 507. (a)(1) Chapter 45 of title 10, United States Code, is amended by adding at the end thereof the following new section:

"§ 775. wearing of unobtrusive religious headgear

"A member of the armed forces may wear at any time unobtrusive religious head-gear, such as a skullcap, if the religious observances or practices of that member include the wearing of such headgear, unless such practice would interfere with the performance of particular military duties assigned to that member."...

Mr. SOLARZ. Mr. Chairman, this is a relatively uncontroversial amendment. I believe it is acceptable to the chairman and the distinguished ranking minority member....

The reason I am offering the amendment now is that there was, 2 weeks ago, a court of appeals decision which had the effect of upholding an Air Force regulation which prohibited a member of the Air Force from wearing a yarmulke while on duty, even though it obviously did not interfere with the performance of his duties.

This seemed to me to be a violation of his first amendment rights....

This amendment does not sanction the wearing of saffron robes or any bizarre religious garments.... The possibility that such a law could be utilized to permit weird forms of clothing is most attenuated.

Mr. WILSON. Will the gentleman yield?

Mr. SOLARZ. Of course I yield to my good friend from Texas.

Mr. WILSON. The gentleman may not be aware of it, but I have a large Indian reservation in my district. I am curious to know if this would apply to war bonnets, unobtrusive, if the warriors felt that they would fight with more ferocity.

Mr. SOLARZ. If a war bonnet would be deemed unobtrusive—

Mr. WILSON. Who does the deeming?

Mr. SOLARZ. In my part of the country they would be fairly obtrusive. But that would be a determination made by the military.

Let me say to the gentleman if they wanted to wear a war bonnet because they thought it would help them fight more effectively, they are not protected by my amendment. They are only affected if this is a religious obligation or requirement or custom or practice, and then only if it is unobtrusive and if it does not interfere with the performance of their duties.

Mr. WILSON. Does the gentleman not see a complication in determining whether or not this is cultural or a religious war bonnet?

For instance, there are Indian tribes that claim the right to use peyote because it has a religious context.

Mr. SOLARZ. Let me ask the gentleman to yield in turn to ask him if the peyote is used as headgear.

Mr. WILSON. No, it is not. But I was using that as an example of an Indian claiming the right to use peyote because of a religious connotation, and the same thing might well be true of a war bonnet.

Mr. SOLARZ. If the gentleman would like to protect the right of Indians to smoke peyote, or whatever else it is you do with peyote, he is free to offer a peyote amendment. This is an unobtrusive headgear amendment. All it refers to is skull caps. It has nothing to do with peyote. And if the gentleman wants to handle peyote, he can handle peyote, but this has nothing to do with peyote.

Mr. WILSON. Will the gentleman accept an amendment to his amendment which would protect my Indians if they do so choose to wear feathers?

Mr. SOLARZ. No, I do not think so. I think that should be considered separately. I would not want to handicap this very carefully drawn amendment which has the approval I think of the committee with this excess baggage.

Does the gentleman know of anybody in an Indian tribe who smokes peyote who is in the armed services?

Mr. WILSON. No, no; those are west Texas Indians that smoke peyote, east Texas Indians do not smoke peyote, but they do wear feathers.

Mr. SOLARZ. Right, but are they in the armed services?

Mr. WILSON. Yes, very patriotic.

Mr. SOLARZ. Have any of them been denied the right to use peyote in the armed services?

Mr. WILSON. No, but they have been denied the right to wear feathers into battle, not like the Italian army, I might add.

— Reps. Stephen J. Solarz (D-N.Y.) and Charles Wilson (D-Tex.)
May 24, 1984

IN REGARD TO THE EXPOSTULATION

Mr. BARKLEY. I wish to say, in regard to the expostulation of the Senator from Missouri—

Mr. DONNELL. Mr. President, I object to the word "expostulation." I have a right to express myself on the floor.

Mr. BARKLEY. The Senator is talking—

Mr. DONNELL. I object to the word "expostulation."

Mr. BARKLEY. Well, go on and object.

Mr. DONNELL. I am objecting now.

Mr. BARKLEY. I am not yielding any further to the Senator from Missouri.

The PRESIDING OFFICER. The Senator from Kentucky.

Mr. BARKLEY. If the Senator does not like the word "expostulation," which is a perfectly good English word, he has a right to object to it.

Mr. DONNELL. I object to any slighting language.

Mr. BARKLEY. The Senator is expostulating, and when anybody expostulates, he is indulging in expostulation.

—Sens. Alben W. Barkley (D-Ky.) and Forrest C. Donnell (R-Mo.)
date unknown

JOKERS WILD

Mr. UNDERWOOD. As I said, I possibly can not illustrate to my friend from Arkansas or my friend from Idaho, because they may not know the game.

Mr. ROBINSON of Arkansas. To what game does the Senator from Alabama refer?

Mr. UNDERWOOD. I am going to explain it right now. If the Senator will take his seat in my chair, I can explain it to him right here.

Mr. ROBINSON of Arkansas. I think just at this time I should prefer to occupy my own chair. [Laughter.]

Mr. UNDERWOOD. There is a game called draw poker—

Mr. SHORTRIDGE of California. One moment, Mr. President. [Laughter.]

Mr. ROBINSON of Arkansas. Mr. President—

Mr. OVERMAN. The Senator will have to explain what that means.

Mr. UNDERWOOD. I am going to illustrate, if my friends will allow me.

Mr. SHORTRIDGE and Mr. ROBINSON of Arkansas addressed the Chair.

The VICE PRESIDENT. The Senator from Alabama has the floor. To whom does the Senator yield?

Mr. UNDERWOOD. I yield first to the Senator from California.

Mr. SHORTRIDGE. The Supreme Court of the State of Kentucky has decided that it is not a game of chance, but purely a scientific undertaking.

Mr. UNDERWOOD. It was in this instance. Now, I yield to the Senator from Arkansas.

Mr. ROBINSON of Arkansas. Mr. President, the Senator from Alabama may draw the fire of the Senator from California by a reference to that mysterious amusement which he calls draw poker, but I assure him that most of us have no knowledge whatever of the subject. [Laughter.]

Mr. UNDERWOOD. I was sure of that, and therefore I excluded my friend from Arkansas.

Mr. ROBINSON of Arkansas. May I ask the Senator from Alabama a question?

Mr. UNDERWOOD. Yes.

Mr. ROBINSON of Arkansas. The Senator from Alabama, I assume, is an expert on the subject he is now discussing?

Mr. UNDERWOOD. I always try to be candid with my friends, and I am not afraid to say what I believe. I have played the game of draw poker. I regret to say that I am not an expert. That has been forcibly illustrated to me. [Laughter.]

Mr. COPELAND. Mr. President, I understood that the Senator from Alabama was going to explain this game to the Senate.

Mr. UNDERWOOD. I am, if I may have the floor.

Mr. NORRIS. Mr. President, the Senator would have to have something else besides the floor.

Mr. CARAWAY. Mr. President—

Mr. UNDERWOOD. I yield, but I should be glad if I might be allowed to proceed.

Mr. CARAWAY. I merely wanted to remark that that is the first time the Senator got the interest of the other side of the Chamber, when he commenced on that subject. [Laughter.]

Mr. UNDERWOOD. To be sure. I realize fully, I will say to my friend from Arkansas, that I now have the most vivid interest of the Senate that I have ever possessed since I have been a Member of this body.

Mr. NORRIS. That only illustrates that the Senators on this side are anxious and willing to learn from those on the other side.

Mr. UNDERWOOD. Yes.

Mr. ROBINSON of Arkansas. And that—

> Where ignorance is bliss
> 'Tis folly to be wise.

Mr. UNDERWOOD. Yes.

Mr. SHORTRIDGE. Mr. President, may I interrupt the Senator for a question?

Mr. UNDERWOOD. I yield.

Mr. SHORTRIDGE. I would like to ask the Senator from Alabama whether three of a kind would beat two pair. [Laughter.]

Mr. UNDERWOOD. I am going to illustrate that right now.

Mr. REED of Missouri. Mr. President, what astonishes me is the interest the Senator from Nebraska has manifested in this subject. [Laughter.]

Mr. UNDERWOOD. If I may come back to the illustration, I think Senators will understand it, even the gentlemen who do not know the game. The old game of draw poker had certain definite rules and regulations as to what was the highest hand. I believe what was called a straight flush was the highest hand available.

SEVERAL SENATORS. A royal flush! [Laughter.]

Mr. UNDERWOOD. A royal flush. But as times progressed, and we reached the age of modern times and modern ideas, innovations were introduced into the game, such as allowing deuces to run wild; I believe that is the term. If a man got a deuce, he could call it an ace, or a king, or anything else. And there were a number of other innovations. Finally the game got to a point where a man could hold innumerable aces and straight flushes, until the game became so confusing that no man knew what he was playing. I do not believe in that kind of innovations. I believe if people are going to play the game, they ought to play it according to the old rules that are laid down in Hoyle, the demonstrated rules.

Mr. REED of Missouri. Then why does the Senator want to change the old rules of the Senate? I think we have an illustration here not of deuces running wild but of a very fine ace running wild. [Laughter.]

—*Sens. Oscar L. Underwood (D-Ala.), Joseph T. Robinson (D-Ark.), Samuel M. Shortridge (R-Calif.) Lee S. Overman (D-N.C.), Royal S. Copeland (D-N.Y.), George W. Norris (R-Nebr.), Thaddeus H. Caraway (D-Ark.), and James A. Reed (D-Mo.)*
June 4, 1926

THEY
DON'T CALL HIM
PRUNE
FACE
FOR
NOTHING

And Other Grand Slams

THEY
DON'T CALL HIM
PRUNE
FACE
FOR
NOTHING

AS I LAY DYING

Mr. BURKE of Massachusetts. Mr. Speaker, I take this time to announce to the Members of the House that a little article appeared in the Boston Sunday Globe yesterday, a script that said I dyed my hair brown. Now, the fellow that wrote this story, I understand, is known as Prune Face and they do not call him Prune Face for nothing. He has more wrinkles than an unmade bed. He must be a little bit jealous of me because of my youthful appearance. I would like to give him a formula to regain his youth; that is, have oatmeal every morning and put a spoonful of molasses in that oatmeal about once a week. It is better than Geritol. No, I do not use any dye formula in my hair although it might help Prune Face. The years have not been too kind to him. He is a lot younger than I but his friend tells me he looks a lot older. Jealousy is an awful trait. However, I forgive old wrinkles. I know he did not intend to be this far removed from the truth.

Mr. HAYS of Ohio. Mr. Speaker, will the gentleman yield?

Mr. BURKE of Massachusetts. I yield to the gentleman from Ohio.

Mr. HAYS of Ohio. Mr. Speaker, what is the Boston Globe?

Mr. BURKE of Massachusetts. The Boston Globe is an outstanding and well-known newspaper up in my area. It has been known down through the years for its integrity.

Mr. HAYS of Ohio. Is it slipping a little?

Mr. BURKE of Massachusetts. I think in this particular case it slipped a little.

Maybe I should strike out that part about the gentleman being prune-faced, Mr. Speaker. I do not want to say that about him. It is an unkind remark to make about him, because he is not a bad fellow. He just has problems every time he looks at me. He is 20 years younger and he looks 10 years older. I am 65 years of age and I am proud of it, never denied it and everybody in my district knows it; but I can say one thing, I have never dyed my hair and I can tell him another thing and I do not know whether he can make the same statement; I still have my own teeth.

> *—Reps. James A. Burke (D-Mass.) and Wayne L. Hays (D-Ohio)*
> *March 1, 1976*

STICKY SUBJECT

Mr. LOTT. Mr. Speaker, when you go to the grocery store, do you nearly "drop your false teeth" over the outrageous prices you must pay? Perhaps you drop your teeth because you cannot afford the denture adhesive to hold them in anymore. At $2.89 a tube, denture adhesive is beginning to look like a luxury.

What is most disheartening is remembering 25 years ago when prices were about a third what they are now. That same tube of denture adhesive sold for 98 cents then, and a person could afford to keep his choppers in his mouth....

> *— Rep. Trent Lott (R-Miss.)*
> *March 10, 1980*

TIPPING THE SCALES

Mr. HELMS. One final note, Mr. President, and I will be finished. What we really have here is a confrontation between TIP O'NEILL and the U.S. Senate....

We sent that bill over to the House and Mr. O'NEILL sat on it. And when Mr. O'NEILL sits on a bill that is a lot of coverage. [Laughter.]

> *—Sen. Jesse Helms (R-N.C.)*
> *March 30, 1982*

LONG WINDED

Mr. LONG. Very well. I will not yield it, but I was hoping that, by unanimous consent, we could find out about it. I want to find out how popular I am in this body. [Laughter.] I want to know. If it should get back to Louisiana that the Senators are sitting here this evening listening to me, after I had been speaking for 7 hours—

Mr. ASHURST. Mr. President, will the Senator yield to me?

The VICE PRESIDENT. Does the Senator from Louisiana yield to the Senator from Arizona?

Mr. LONG. I yield for a question.

Mr. ASHURST. I can answer the Senator as to his popularity at this moment, but I do not want to take him off the floor.

Mr. LA FOLLETTE. Mr. President, I make the point of order that the Senator from Arizona is not asking a question.

The VICE PRESIDENT. The point of order is well taken.

Mr. LONG. I only yield for a question; but I want to say that when the news gets back to Bossum Neck that after having spoken for 7 hours there was no Senator who wanted to leave, it will mean that my standing will have gone up 100 percent.

Mr. ASHURST. Mr. President, a parliamentary inquiry.

The VICE PRESIDENT. The Senator will state it.

Mr. ASHURST. Is it not true that the Senator's present popularity is about as great as that of a cuckoo clock in a boys' dormitory at 3 o'clock in the morning?

The VICE PRESIDENT. The Chair is not prepared to answer the parliamentary inquiry. Each Senator must answer in his own conscience how popular the Senator from Louisiana is.

> —*Sens. Huey P. Long (D-La.), Henry F. Ashurst (D-Ariz.), and*
> *Robert M. La Follette, Jr. (R-Wis.)*
> *June 13, 1935*

THAT CLEARS THINGS UP

Mr. EAGLETON. Mr. President, I always enjoy listening to my good friend, the Senator from Pennsylvania. He is able, he is articulate, and he can be, when he is at his best, obfuscating.

> — *Sen. Thomas F. Eagleton (D-Mo.) [on Senator Hugh Scott (R-Pa.)]*
> *October 1, 1974*

TURKEY-GOBBLER STRUT

Pity poor Roscoe Conkling, a Democratic Representative from New York who, in April 1866, had the misfortune of finding himself the target of Speaker James G. Blaine's wrath. Blaine's powerful oratorical salvos followed two days of bitter, personal debate between the two over the Army Reorganization Bill. Conkling never recovered from them. He carried to his grave a burning hatred of Blaine, who had forever branded him as the man with the "turkey- gobbler strut."
Here are excerpts from Blaine's blistering attack:

Mr. BLAINE. Mr. Speaker—
The SPEAKER. Does the gentleman from New York yield to the gentleman from Maine?
Mr. CONKLING. No, sir. I do not wish to have anything to do with the member from Maine, not even so much as to yield him the floor.
Mr. BLAINE. All right.
*Mr. CONKLING....*Now, Mr. Speaker, one thing further: if the member from Maine had the least idea how profoundly indifferent I am to his opinion upon the subject which he has been discussing, or upon any other subject personal to me, I think he would hardly take the trouble to rise here and express his opinion. And as it is a matter of entire indifference to me what that opinion may be, I certainly will not detain the House by discussing the question whether it is well or ill founded, or by noticing what he says....
*Mr. BLAINE....*As to the gentleman's cruel sarcasm, I hope he will not be too severe. The contempt of that large-minded gentleman is so wilting; his haughty disdain, his grandeloquent swell, his majestic, supereminent,

overpowering, turkey-gobbler strut has been so crushing to myself and all the members of this House that I know it was an act of the greatest temerity for me to venture upon a controversy with him. But, sir, I know who is responsible for all this. I know that within the last few weeks, as members of the House will recollect, an extra strut has characterized the gentleman's bearing. It is not his fault. It is the fault of another. That gifted and satirical writer, Theodore Tilton, of the New York Independent, spent some weeks recently in this city. His letters published in that paper embraced, with many serious statements, a little jocose satire, a part of which was the statement that the mantle of the late Winter Davis had fallen upon the member from New York. The gentleman took it seriously, and it has given his strut additional pomposity. The resemblance is great. It is striking. Hyperion to a satyr, Thersites to Hercules, mud to marble, dunghill to diamond, a singed cat to a Bengal tiger, a whining puppy to a roaring lion. Shade of the mighty Davis, forgive the almost profanation of that jocose satire!

— Reps. Roscoe Conkling (D-N.Y.) and James G. Blaine (R-Maine)
The Congressional Globe, April 30, 1866

IDIOT'S DELIGHT

Mr. HAYS of Ohio. The gentleman is making a ridiculous request.

Mr. BAUMAN. I am serious.

Mr. HAYS of Ohio. The gentleman is not serious at all. The gentleman and I both know it, but if the gentleman wants to get specific about places where we did make money I will talk about it, but I will not engage in exercises in idiocy.

Mr. BAUMAN. The gentleman is aptly qualified to judge idiocy.

— Reps. Wayne L. Hays (D-Ohio) and Robert E. Bauman (R-Md.)
May 6, 1975

INQUIRING MINDS

Mr. FRANK. Mr. Speaker, will the gentleman yield?
Mr. WALKER. I am very glad to yield.

PARLIAMENTARY INQUIRY

Mr. FRANK. Mr. Speaker, I have a parliamentary inquiry.
The SPEAKER pro tempore. Will the gentleman from Pennsylvania (Mr. WALKER) yield for the purpose of a parliamentary inquiry?
Mr. WALKER. I yield to the gentleman from Massachusetts. I thought he had a question or a statement.
Mr. FRANK. I have a parliamentary inquiry.
Mr. WALKER. I yield for a parliamentary inquiry.
The SPEAKER pro tempore. The gentleman will state his parliamentary inquiry.
Mr. FRANK. The parliamentary inquiry is dealing with the question of propriety. Is the term "crybaby" an appropriate phrase to be used in a debate in the House?
The SPEAKER pro tempore. The Chair would hope that the phrase would not be used.
Mr. FRANK. I thank the Speaker.

—Reps. Robert S. Walker (R-Pa.) and Barney Frank (D-Mass.)
May 31, 1984

ROCKY

Mr. JACOBS. Mr. Speaker, this past weekend at a fundraising dinner for Vice President ROCKEFELLER, President Ford said it is easier to negotiate with our country's adversaries than to negotiate with the Congress.

The audience howled its delight.

Me, too.

I mean, after all, this is the administration that negotiated the Russian wheat deal.

Speaking of Congress, is not a fundraiser for a Rockefeller somewhat incongruous?

— Rep. Andrew Jacobs, Jr. (D-Ind.)
February 19, 1975

SHORT SUBJECT

Mr. McKELLAR. Mr. President, will the Senator yield?

Mr. BARKLEY. I yield.

Mr. McKELLAR. Does the Senator know of any such case as that? I have never heard of it. Of course, I have not been here as long as has the Senator from Kentucky.

Mr. BARKLEY. The Senator from Tennessee came to Congress when I was in knee pants. [Laughter.] He came to the Senate at least 10 years before I became a member of the Senate.

Mr. McKELLAR. The Senator was down in the woods of Kentucky. I do not know what sort of breeches he wore, but he was a big boy then. [Laughter.]

Will the Senator yield to me for something serious?

... Some question was raised here about the ages of two Senators, I being one and the Senator from Kentucky [Mr. BARKLEY] the other. The Senator from Kentucky made the astounding statement that when I was in the House of Representatives a good many years ago, he was a boy in short breeches. I wish to read from the Congressional Directory the biographical sketch of the Senator. He was born in Graves County, Ky., November 24, 1877. I went to the House in 1911. Therefore, when my distinguished friend was wearing short breeches, he was just 34 years of age. I am utterly astounded that, though he came from Graves County, Ky., in the country, he should have been wearing short trousers—short breeches—at that time. [Laughter.]

Mr. BARKLEY. Short pants.

Mr. McKELLAR. Thirty-four years old and wearing short breeches! The remarkable thing about it is that the very next year he was elected to the House of Representatives. I wonder whether he was in short breeches when he came to the House of Representatives in 1913.

Mr. BARKLEY. If the Senator will yield in that connection, I have never denied my age. It is in the directory, where everyone can see it. I have searched in vain to find in the directory the age of my very dear friend, the Senator from Tennessee.

Mr. McKELLAR. Mr. President, I received hundreds of letters of congratulations and innumerable telegrams just a few days ago when I celebrated my birthday.

Mr. BARKLEY. How old was the Senator?

Mr. McKELLAR. Seventy-five years old, and the Senator is 9 years younger than I am.

Mr. BARKLEY. I move, therefore, to insert in the biographical section of the Congressional Directory the date of the birth of the Senator from Tennessee.

The ACTING PRESIDENT pro tempore. Is there objection? The Chair hears none.

Mr. BARKLEY. Getting back to short pants, I merely wish to say that when I came to the House of Representatives in 1913 at the age of 34, I was in long pants, but the Senator from Tennessee has been trying to pull them off me or shorten them ever since. [Laughter.]

—Sens. Kenneth D. McKellar (D-Tenn.) and Alben W. Barkley (D-Ky.)
February 10, 1944

PLANE FACTS

Mr. HAYS of Ohio. Mr. Speaker, I had the rare opportunity to go over my morning's mail this morning when it came in, and I am sure many Members have not, but I suppose in their mail they will find a communication, as I did, from Frank Borman, president of Eastern Airlines, in which he informs us he has requested an increase in the fares of 1 percent this month and 2 percent a month for the several months to come.

I replied to Mr. Borman this morning and told him it had been my misfortune through an error on the part of one of my staff to be booked on Eastern Airlines to Miami last Tuesday. I had never been on a dirtier airplane with ruder personnel in my life.

I was in the first-class section which had been reconverted from tourist. It had not been very well reconverted. As far as the food I was served, I am sorry I did not have any hogs on my farm because I would have saved that food and taken it home to them.

This friend and I were assigned the two front seats and were told to put our baggage under the seat in front of us, and there was not any seat in front of us. My friend said he was ready to get off and I was, too, but one of the hostesses found a space for us to put our baggage in.

I proposed to Mr. Borman that before the fare increase he ought to: First, clean up the airlines; second, get their people to be polite; third, give better service; and, if he cannot do those three things I suggest he might want to return to the Moon and stay there....

— Rep. Wayne L. Hays (D-Ohio)
January 19, 1976

RIGHT AND WRONG

Mr. McKELLAR. Mr. President, in carrying out my conscientious views I greatly regret that it is sometimes necessary for me to vote on the same side with the Senator from Louisiana [Laughter]; but when I do so, I wish to assure the Senator from Louisiana that it makes me feel doubtful of my own position. I think I must be wrong in some way when I find myself voting on the same side with the Senator from Louisiana, because I know the Senator is so generally wrong that I can hardly believe he is right at any time. [Laughter in the galleries.]

— Sen. Kenneth D. McKellar (D-Tenn.)[on Sen. Huey P. Long (D-La.)]
June 13, 1935

THURSDAY EVENING DISCUSSION

Mr. GROSS. May I ask the gentleman from Massachusetts whether there is another golf tournament next Monday, as there was on last Tuesday, or why is not some of this stuff down here at the end of the program for next week elevated to Monday of next week?

Mr. O'NEILL. I will be happy to answer that. One of the frailties of the leadership on both sides of the aisle is that they like to try to protect the Members if they possibly can. In view of the fact that there are seven primaries on that day, we thought it was the decent and fair thing to set the schedule up in this manner.... I know the gentleman appreciates what we are trying to do.

Mr. GROSS. The gentleman from Iowa likes to be charitable—

Mr. O'NEILL. I am happy to hear that.

Mr. GROSS (continuing). But some of us around here at least go through the motions of seeing to it that this place runs. If no one is here at all, it is not going to run.

Mr. O'NEILL. I am sure the gentleman has not gone through just motions. He is a very effective Congressman—and we all know it.

Mr. ARENDS. If the gentleman will yield, I might say to the gentleman from Iowa that I am not worried about whether this place is going to run next week; I am worried about when the gentleman is gone next year, and I am gone, too, whether this place is going to run....

Mr. O'NEILL. I just want to say to the gentleman that come next year, I will miss these Thursday evening discussions.

Mr. GROSS. I hope the gentleman does not drown in his sorrow.

—*Reps. H.R. Gross (R-Iowa), Thomas P. (Tip) O'Neill, Jr. (D-Mass.), and Leslie C. Arends (R-Ill.)*
May 30, 1974

C.R.A.P.

Mr. SYMMS. If the gentleman will yield further, I will say to the gentleman that I will not object to this measure, but I will say that we all know what the initials of the constructive Republican alternative proposals spell, and I feel that this is really what we really have here.

Mr. BROWN of Michigan. The gentleman is justified in characterizing it in any way he wants to.

—*Reps. Steven D. Symms (R-Idaho) and Garry E. Brown (R-Mich.)*
June 26, 1975

IT'S ALL GREEK

Mr. BARKLEY. Mr. President, will the Senator yield?

Mr. LONG. I yield for a question.

Mr. BARKLEY. The Senator has been making a very able and persuasive address, and I think he has persuaded us that we ought to vote for his motion to reconsider. Will he let us vote on his motion, now that he has convinced us of its wisdom?

Mr. LONG. If the Senator from Kentucky announces he is in favor of the motion, I am going to withdraw it. I want the Senator to think very carefully; because if I find out that after mature deliberation the Senator from Kentucky is going to vote for my motion, I will know it is wrong and I shall withdraw the motion. [Laughter.]

The PRESIDING OFFICER. The Chair again admonishes the occupants of the galleries against any demonstration of approval or disapproval.

Mr. LONG.....The only time that I have ever seen the Senator vote right in my life was when I told him in advance how I was going to vote, and he voted that way by accident.

Mr. BARKLEY. If I voted the way the Senator did it was by accident. [Laughter.]

Mr. LONG. The only time I ever voted wrong in this body—and I had to apologize to the president occupant of the chair, who criticized me for it—was the time when I let the Senator from Kentucky advise me. [Laughter.] ...

Mr. LEWIS. Mr. President, will the Senator yield?

Mr. LONG. I yield.

Mr. LEWIS. Having been absent on official business, I do not know exactly to what motion the able Senator from Louisiana refers, though I must say that, so far as I am concerned, I regard it as continual motion and the Senator as perpetual action.

Mr. BARKLEY. Mr. President, will the Senator yield?

Mr. LONG. For a question only.

Mr. LEWIS. Mr. President, I was going to ask my able friend a question, who, as I say, I am pleased to recognize at any time as perpetual motion. What is the particular motion to which he now alludes on which he says he desires to have the support of the Senator from Kentucky?

Mr. LONG. I will state to the Senator that I have been delivering a lecture on the Constitution. For the last hour of my time I have devoted my remarks to a lecture on the Constitution of the United States.

Mr. LEWIS. I am afraid I regard that as a foreign subject at this particular time. [Laughter.]

Mr. LONG. That is what I was afraid of. I had just made the remark that it was a vanished subject. But we love to talk about the myths of Greece. Grecian mythology is the most engaging of all subjects. Nothing is so interesting as the tale of the wooden horse that was dragged to the gates of Troy.

Mr. BARKLEY. I thought the whole horse got in, not simply the tail. [Laughter.]

Mr. LONG. The horse did get in. The horse probably had things around it like those the Senator from Kentucky might be thinking of.

Mr. BARKLEY. But it did not have anything in it like what the Senator from Louisiana has in him. [Laughter.]

Mr. LONG. I do not suppose it did. We love to read of ancient Greece, or the history of Troy. I do not read Greek—

Mr. BARKLEY. But the Senator talks a lot of it.

Mr. LONG. And I do not even know how to read Latin now. I do know some Latin sayings. I got it all for half a dollar in my early life. However, these things which are foreign, these things which are ancient, these things which are more or less a matter of mythology, are engaging, they are enticing, they are interesting.

I was speaking of the ancient and forgotten lore of the Constitution. Even love is not more bewitching than a discussion of its vanishing precepts. That is why I bring them up so that I may interest some in them. So for the past hour I have been devoting my remarks to a lecture on the Constitution.

As will be recalled by my friend the Senator from Illinois [Mr. LEWIS], who either has read all these things about Troy, or helped to write them, I do not know which. [Laughter.] They dragged a wooden horse right up to the gates of Troy, the Greeks made the Trojans a present of him, and the Trojans carried the wooden horse inside. What they did with the horse after they got it inside I do not know but the horse was there, and we have spent a lot of time talking about that wooden horse. It is the best understood thing there is in the schoolroom today, and my only hope now is to interest the young, rising manhood of this country in the forgotten articles of the Constitution of the United States by arousing in their minds an attraction to these things which are mythical, which are vanishing, and which depend upon tradition for their perpetuity....

The intense interest which is being manifested in my speech here causes me to proceed with almost undue caution, and I feel almost impelled to request Senators to restrain themselves lest they applaud me as I proceed with my lecture on this question....

Where does this lead us? I want to say that if the members of the Senate would stay here and listen to me we would correct these conditions. Here I am making this speech on these facts, about which the Members of the Senate do not know a thing—95 percent of them know nothing about them at all, because they have not listened to me. [Laughter.] Here I am with 14 Senators listening to one of the greatest speeches that has ever been made in this body. [Laughter.] I cannot get them to listen. Again, when we do get them to listen, half of them are like the Senator from Kentucky—they cannot understand the speech after they hear it. [Laughter.]

Mr. BARKLEY. Mr. President—

The PRESIDING OFFICER (Mr. MURPHY in the chair). Does the Senator from Louisiana yield to the Senator from Kentucky?

Mr. LONG. I yield.

Mr. BARKLEY. I am not responsible for the Senator's inability to make himself understood. [Laughter.]

Mr. LONG. Very well. I had that coming to me. I remember when I first tried to study music; they gave me a very poor grade.

Mr. BARKLEY. Did the Senator learn music?

Mr. LONG. Not much of it; a little.

Mr. BARKLEY. Will not the Senator sing a little? [Laughter.]

Mr. LONG. Mr. President, the Senator wants me to sing to him. There may be some people I will sing to, but they will be better looking than the Senator from Kentucky. [Laughter.]

Mr. BARKLEY. The Senator will never sing looking in the looking glass, then, if that be true.

—Sen. Alben W. Barkley (D-Ky.), Huey P. Long (D-La.), and
James H. Lewis (D-Wash.)
June 13, 1935

I'LL HUG YOUR ELEPHANT IF YOU KISS MY A--

Democrats vs. Republicans

I'LL HUG
YOUR
ELEPHANT
IF YOU
KISS MY A--

VIVA LA DIFFERENCE

Mr. JACOBS. Mr. Speaker, the following is circa early 1960's, but it probably remains about right.

TO BE READ ALOUD BY A DEMOCRAT TO A REPUBLICAN
OR BY A REPUBLICAN TO A DEMOCRAT

Although to the casual glance Republicans and Democrats may appear to be almost indistinguishable, here are some hints which should result in positive identification:

Democrats seldom make good polo players. They would rather listen to Bela Bartok.

The people you see coming out of white wooden churches are Republicans.

Democrats buy most of the books that have been banned somewhere. Republicans form censorship committees and read them as a group.

Republicans are likely to have fewer but larger debts that cause them no concern. Democrats owe a lot of small bills. They don't worry either.

Republicans consume three-fourths of all the rutabaga produced in this country. The remainder is thrown out.

Republicans usually wear hats and almost always clean their paintbrushes.

Democrats give their worn-out clothes to those less fortunate. Republicans wear theirs.

Republicans post all the signs saying No Trespassing and These Deer are Private Property and so on. Democrats bring picnic baskets and start their bonfires with signs.

Republicans employ exterminators. Democrats step on the bugs.

Republicans have governesses for their children. Democrats have grandmothers.

Democrats name their children after currently popular sports figures, politicians and entertainers. Republican children are named after their parents or grandparents, according to where the most money is.

Large cities such as New York are filled with Republicans—up until 5 p.m. At this point there is a phenomenon much like an automatic washer starting the spin cycle. People begin pouring out of every exit of the city. These are Republicans going home.

Democrats keep trying to cut down on smoking, but are not successful. Neither are Republicans.

Republicans tend to keep their shades drawn, although there is seldom any reason why they should. Democrats ought to, but don't.

Republicans fish from the stern of a chartered boat. Democrats sit on the dock and let the fish come to them.

Republicans study the financial pages of the newspaper. Democrats put them in the bottom of the bird cage.

Most of the stuff you see alongside the road has been thrown out of car windows by Democrats.

On Saturday, Republicans head for the hunting lodge or the yacht club. Democrats wash the car and get a haircut.

Republicans raise dahlias, Dalmatians and eyebrows. Democrats raise Airedales, kids and taxes.

Democrats eat the fish they catch. Republicans hang them on the wall.

Democrats watch TV crime and Western shows that make them clench their fists and become red in the face. Republicans get the same effect from the presidential press conferences.

Christmas cards that Democrats send are filled with reindeer and chimneys and long messages. Republicans select cards containing a spray of holly, or a single candle.

Democrats are continually saying, "This Christmas we're going to be sensible." Republicans consider this highly unlikely.

Republicans smoke cigars on weekdays.

Republicans have guest rooms. Democrats have spare rooms filled with old baby furniture.

Republican boys date Democratic girls. They plan to marry Republican girls, but feel they're entitled to a little fun first.

Democrats make up plans and then do something else. Republicans follow the plans their grandfathers made.

Democrats purchase all the tools—the power saws and mowers. A Republican probably wouldn't know how to use a screwdriver.

Democrats suffer from chapped hands and headaches. Republicans have tennis elbow and gout.

Republicans sleep in twin beds—some even in separate rooms. That is why there are more Democrats.

— Rep. Andrew Jacobs, Jr. (D-Ind.)
July 19, 1983

STEADY AS SHE GOES

Mr. HUGH SCOTT. I thank the distinguished majority leader. I think we all agree that he is the fairest man we know.

Mr. PASTORE. And a Democrat, at that.

Mr. HUGH SCOTT. He is more than a Democrat. He is a very good American, and I want to be able to say that about all my colleagues on the other side of the aisle, and I am sure I can. But I also hope they will be free to say it about us, because we are in the same country, we are in the same boat, and we are in a hell of a mess.

Mr. PASTORE. That is right. The boat is rocking.

Mr. HUGH SCOTT. Not my boat—your boat.

Mr. PASTORE. Your boat.

Mr. HUGH SCOTT. I hope the Senator from Rhode Island will get off his partisan bias here and stand somewhere in the middle of the boat.

[Laughter.]

—Sens. Hugh Scott (R-Pa.) and John O. Pastore (D-R.I.)
October 10, 1974

NAILING DOWN VOTES

Mr. DANIELSON. Mr. Speaker, I did not intend to say something but once in a while something wells up within one, and something just welled up.

I want to congratulate the House and all of my wonderful colleagues on the vote by which we passed this last bill. It is terribly important. I think it is absolutely a proper statesmanlike vote in the right direction.

I heard all of those speeches about "This is different; we voted against debt limits before but now we should not vote against them." I believe that all of that is in the category of rubbish and balderdash and rutabagas, but nevertheless this was a good vote. It has been said, and this is important, that any jackass can kick down the barn door but it takes a carpenter to build one. I welcome my friends from the other side of the aisle to the ranks of the carpenters.

—Rep. George E. Danielson (D-Calif.)
February 5, 1981

WHAT IS A CONSERVATIVE?

Mr. JACOBS. Mr. Speaker, well, I think I've finally figured it out.

A Conservative in Russia is one who accuses a Liberal of being soft on capitalism.

A Conservative in America is one who accuses a Liberal of being soft on communism.

A Conservative on the House Education and Labor Committee is one who spends conservatively. A Liberal on the House Education and Labor Committee is one who spends liberally.

A Conservative on the House Armed Services Committee is one who spends liberally. A Liberal on the House Armed Services Committee is one who spends conservatively.

A Conservative in the White House is one who borrows to pay current expenses. A Conservative in business is one who does not borrow to pay current expenses.

So, which you are obviously depends on where you are.

— Rep. Andrew Jacobs, Jr. (D-Ind.)
January 28, 1987

PRACTICE MAKES PREFECT

Mr. DANIELSON. Mr. Speaker, I enjoy this 1-minute period more than anything else in the Congress. One of the things that it demonstrates is the difference between Republicans and Democrats.

Now, the old definition was that the main difference between Republicans and Democrats was that Republicans hired exterminators, whereas Democrats stepped on bugs. But clearly there are some other differences. I have noticed that Republicans come to the well and read speeches that are written for them by somebody else, while Democrats speak from the heart.

I also notice that when Republicans give their speech, they say, "Now, the trouble with the American people is that 'they' are going to do this, and 'they' will have 20/20 vision and 'they' remember 'Fifty-four forty or fight.'"

When Democrats make such speeches, they say, "We." We identify ourselves with the American people, whereas, the Republicans, who have never quite been assimilated into the American society, refer to Americans as being "they."

But anyway, they are practicing a lot lately, these Republicans, and by golly, some of these speeches are good, particularly the one about basketball.

Mr. ASHBROOK. Mr. Speaker, will the gentleman yield?

Mr. DANIELSON. I yield to the gentleman from Ohio.

Mr. ASHBROOK. I thank my colleague and I welcome him to the 1-minute happy hour.

Mr. DANIELSON. Thank you very much. We are all "Minute Men." Bless you all.

> — *Reps. George E. Danielson (D-Calif.) and John M. Ashbrook (R-Ohio)*
> *March 10, 1980*

KINGFISH, CRAWFISH, AND OTHER DELICACIES

*Mr. President,
you roll these oysters
in the dry meal . . .*

KINGFISH,
CRAWFISH,
AND
OTHER DELICACIES

THE HAMBURGER CRISIS

Mr. HAYAKAWA. Mr. President, we are in the midst of a crisis. The Congress has in the past met to consider the prospect of wars in foreign lands, but never have we considered a conflict that strikes so close to the heart of our society as Burger War I. Three of America's biggest burgermeisters—McDonald's, Wendy's, and Burger King—are at this moment taking each other to court to decide whose burger is best.

Before I consider the implications of the struggle itself, I would like to take a moment to pay tribute to the hamburger. No single food, finger licking or mmmm mmmm good, comes close to matching the hamburger in its all-American appeal. Rich or poor, black, white, or brown, we are of one mind when it comes to our national mania. I have never in my 76 years witnessed a station wagon full of little league baseball players pull into a quiche stand or a Hungarian restaurant. Here in our own Senate cafeteria Chinese weeks and pizza Fridays come and go, but the cheeseburger lives on. Simply put, nothing tops a hamburger (although the Senator from Pennsylvania[1] may have some thoughts on the subject).

Except for our shared language, the hamburger is probably the only thing we Americans have in common. This is why I am troubled by the burger war now being waged. An American institution is being sullied as it is dragged through the courts, and I fear that complex legal issues may bewilder harried citizens into foregoing the hamburger entirely. That would indeed be a tragic occurrence.

But, Mr. President, all is not lost. I believe that the good judgment and democratic intuition of the American people will prevail in the end. Even a lawyer cannot deter an American from his favorite food.

So I will say it with relish. Give me a hamburger, Mr. President, but hold the lawsuit.

—Sen. S.I. Hayakawa (R-Calif.)
October 1, 1982

[1]Ed. note: Sen. John Heinz (R-Pa.)

"MR. PRESIDENT, YOU ROLL THESE OYSTERS IN THE DRY MEAL . . ."

Mr. LONG. Mr. President, people up in this part of the country never have learned to fry oysters as well as we have done down our way.

I have spent a number of evenings acquainting people with how to prepare oysters. I had a bucket of oysters sent to me from Louisiana the other night, and I was asked by a very fine bunch of my friends if I would not drop around with the New Orleans oysters and fry some of them for them in good Louisiana style and way. So, Mr. President, I bought a frying pan about 8 inches deep. I bought the frying pan because I was afraid they would not have a frying pan there in which I could fry the oysters. I bought a frying pan, as I said, 8 inches deep and about 17 inches in diameter.

Mr. TYDINGS. Mr. President, will the Senator yield?

Mr. LONG. I yield.

Mr. TYDINGS. When the Senator fries oysters, is pot liquor one of the concomitants?

Mr. LONG. No; that does not go in with the oysters. I will come to that later....

As I was going to illustrate, Mr. President, about these oysters that I got from New Orleans. I bought this frying pan 8 inches deep and 14 to 16 inches or 17 inches in diameter, and I bought a 10-pound bucket of cottonseed-oil lard, but I forgot to get a strainer, and when I got to the place to fry the oysters I had everything there except the meal and the strainer.

The lady had some meal, but she did not have any salt to salt the meal with, and that was the only bad thing about it. The strainer which they had was not the best strainer in the world, but I could use it all right.

However, they had no salt for the meal, but I took the oysters, Mr. President, the way they should be taken, and laid them out on a muslin cloth, about 12 of them, and then you could pull the cloth over and you dry the oysters. You dry them, you see, first with a muslin cloth, and then you take the oysters, after they have been dried, and you roll them into a meal which is salted. I did not have it salted this night, but it should have been salted. [Laughter in the galleries.]

Mr. President, you roll these oysters in the dry meal. You do not want to cook the meal or put water in the meal at any time or anything like that. Just salt the meal and roll the oysters in it. Then, let the grease get boiling hot. You want the grease about 6 inches deep. Then you take the oysters and you place the oysters in the strainer, and you put the strainer in the grease, full depth down to the bottom. Then, you fry those oysters in boiling grease until they turn a gold-copper color and rise to the top, and then, you take them out and let them cool just a little bit before you eat them.

Now, Mr. President, most people cannot tell when an oyster is done. They do not know when it has been fried enough. You wrongfully put them on the bottom of a skillet. You have got to have them totally submerged and you wait until they rise to the top, and when they rise to the top, a golden copper color, then the oyster is cooked just exactly right, and then you take the strainer up out of the grease in the dish and the oysters are there and you let them drip for a little while and allow them to cool a little and then you eat them.

Mr. TYDINGS. Mr. President—

The PRESIDING OFFICER. Does the Senator from Louisiana yield to the Senator from Maryland?

Mr. LONG. I yield.

Mr. TYDINGS. Does the Senator realize when he describes how these oysters are cooked and how appetizing they seem to be, that those of us who are listening are being inhumanly punished? [Laughter.]

Mr. LONG. I had forgotten that. I was trying to make the Senator from Mississippi [Mr. HARRISON] hungry, but he was raised in a part of the country where they do not understand the science of eating anyway. He has left the Chamber. I am afraid I made him hungry.

That is the way to cook oysters. If every Member of the Senate will clip out of the RECORD tomorrow what I have said today and not give it to his wife, but go and do it himself and then teach his wife—learn how to do it himself and then teach his wife—he will know how to fry oysters better than most families in Washington.

There is no telling how many lives have been lost by not knowing how to fry oysters, but serving them as an indigestible food. Many times we hear of some man who was supposed to have had an acute attack of indigestion or cerebral hemorrhage or heart failure, and the chances are the only thing that was the matter with him was that he had swallowed some improperly cooked oysters. [Laughter.]

> *—Sens. Huey P. Long (D-La.) and Millard E. Tydings (D-Md.)*
> *June 13, 1935*

"NOW, I COME TO POT LIKKER . . ."

Mr. LONG. Now, I come to pot likker. Now, I will give my recipe for pot likker. First let me tell Senators what pot likker is. Pot likker is the residue that remains from the commingling, heating, and evaporation [laughter]—any way, it is in the bottom of the pot! [Laughter.]

Here is how pot likker is made. First you get some turnip greens. You have to wash turnip greens many times. One of the principal reasons why people do not like turnip greens is that they never do get them clean. "You have to wash them lots of times," said Cato, "lots of times." They always call him "Cato." [Laughter.]

Take the ordinary green, turnip greens or mustard greens, though turnip greens are better than mustard greens. Turnip greens contain more manganese than do mustard greens. The trouble with turnip greens is that most people never get the greens washed clean. Sand is always in them. You have to wash them and wash them and wash them, particularly if you have not any flowing water. If you have good flowing water to shower them with, you can wash them more easily. But you have to wash them plenty of times. In order to get every vestige of dirt and sand and grit out of the greens you have to wash them many, many times.

That is the first thing you do—wash the greens. You wash the turnip with the greens or you can cut the turnips off and peel them and wash them by themselves, and then wash the greens by themselves if you want to do it that way.

All right this far! Then you take the greens and turnips and put them in the pot. Remember this: Do not salt them. Do not put any salt, do not put any pepper, do not put any mustard, do not put any kind of seasoning in the pot with them. Put the greens in the pot. Cut up the turnips. The turnip greens could be cut up a little, too. Put them all in there together.

Then when you get them all in the pot together, put in a sizable quantity of water, I should say about as much water as you have of turnip greens. Then put in there a piece of salted side meat. I would say if you had a pot of turnip greens about two-thirds the size of this wastebasket which I hold in my hand, or perhaps three-fourths that much, you ought to put about a 1-pound hunk of side meat that is sliced, but not clear through, just down to the skin part. Put about a pound of side meat in there. That side meat is just salty enough and has just salt enough in it that it will properly temper the turnip greens when it has been cooked enough. That will be all the seasoning that is needed.

When you have cooked the greens until they are tender and the turnips until they are tender, then you take up the turnips and the greens, and the soup that is left is pot likker. [Laughter.]

That brings on the real question of the art of eating pot likker, the matter of consuming pot likker. You draw off the pot likker and you eat it separately from the turnip greens.

(At this point Mr. LONG yielded to Mr. McCARRAN, who suggested the absence of a quorum, and the roll was called.)

Mr. LONG. Mr. President, the quorum call discloses a majority of the Members here, and I am glad they are here. Now, I wish to conclude what I am sending out to the neighborhood in general on the recipe.

I was at the point where I explained the cooking of oysters. I was just down to the preparation of "pot likker," and had gotten through the first stages of the explanation of how to prepare "pot likker." I had explained everything except to tell them that the turnip greens must be cooked long enough. One great trouble here is that they never cook the turnip greens long enough. Do not cook them too long but cook them long enough. Do not steam them. You have to boil them.

I have stated those recipes for the RECORD this afternoon so that they may be had by all Members of the Senate and by the public at large tomorrow. Now that so many Senators have returned, I am no longer talking for the benefit of the RECORD. I am talking now for the benefit of the Senate because I have Senators here. I was speaking to the country a moment ago. The remarks I made were intended more for the country than for the Senate. Of course, I intended them for the Senate, too, but I intended them more for the country than I did for the Senate.

— Sen. Huey P. Long (D-La.)
June 13, 1935

"YOU TAKE A FORK AND YOU MASH THE ROQUEFORT CHEESE..."

Mr. LONG. Of course, as I have previously told this body, had they not purchased the Louisiana Territory we would not have had the State of Iowa, and we would not have had the Senator from Iowa [Mr. MURPHY] here. We might have been able to do without him. We would not have had here the Senators from Kansas. We might have been able to do without them. We would not have had here the Senators from Oklahoma. We might have been able to do without them. We would not have had here the Senators from Missouri. We might have been able to do without them. But we would not have had the Senator from Louisiana here tonight if Jefferson had not bought the Louisiana Purchase Territory. I will leave it to the Senate what that would have meant to the country. [Laughter.]

Yes, sir; I will leave it to the impartial judgment of the Senate as to what it would have meant if Louisiana had not been brought into the Union. That is an important matter—the State of Louisiana.

Mr. President, I came near forgetting something tonight. I was giving the recipes 5 hours ago. It is now 11 o'clock. I was just going to say that I had one more recipe that I wish to get into the CONGRESSIONAL RECORD. One of my very most famous recipes is not in the RECORD. I want every man who buys the CONGRESSIONAL RECORD tomorrow or day after tomorrow to be able to get in one copy everything he needs to know about the Government, if I can put it in the RECORD. In other words, I am writing a new textbook on government, and I am including in it a few of my favorite cooking recipes, so that I shall not be bothered and pestered by the people up here in the East who are constantly asking me to come around and show them how to cook these articles. I do not want to be said to be discourteous to these people. I do not want them to think I am selfish. I am willing that they shall know what I know.

I have already put into the RECORD the recipe for frying oysters, and the recipe for "pot likker." I wonder if we could not print these recipes as a Senate document and send them out separately. If we would print two or three million copies, Mr. President, and send them out, and give every Member of the Senate free a hundred thousand copies to send out, it would do an immense amount of good. It would do an untold amount of good. But I will put in my third recipe. I will wait until tomorrow—I have only an hour to wait, and I will wait until tomorrow—to discuss with Members of this body about whether or not there should be a separate Senate document to cover these recipes.

The third recipe I am going to give is on how to make Roquefort cheese salad dressing. There were only two men in the United States who understood how to make it, and I knew how to make it better than the other man, and the other man is dead, anyway [laughter]; so I will now give the recipe.

You take a quantity of cheese, say a pound. It depends upon how many people you want to make salad dressing for. Let us say there are three or four people. They ought not to consume over a pound of Roquefort cheese. You take that Roquefort cheese, and you take a fork. Do not take anything but a fork. Do not take a knife. Do not take a potato masher or anything like that. That will not do the work. You take a fork, and you mash the Roquefort cheese into a consistency that is soluble. You thoroughly mash the cheese to a point where there is not an unbroken particle in it. Then you put in olive oil. For a pound of cheese you ought to put in somewhere around three tablespoonsful of olive oil; but you cannot go exactly on the quantity by measurement. You have to be a good judge of cooking. You have to be able to tell when it is mixed to the point of a good consistency. You get that by experience. It gets to be a little bit fluffylike, spongelike; and you mix the olive oil until it is thoroughly mixed, well mixed. It takes a lot of stirring. Any good cooking takes a lot of stirring and lots of mixing. That is what I learned. You have to do lots of stirring and lots of mixing in any good cooking. It takes work to be a good cook.

When you have thoroughly mixed the olive oil with the cheese—it takes about 5 minutes of stirring—then you put in vinegar. If you put in the vinegar before the olive oil, or put in the olive oil before the vinegar, you will ruin the dish. You have to mix them in the right order. Then you put in about two tablespoonsful of vinegar; but, again, you cannot go by exact measurement. You have to put just as much as the cheese will dissolve, and as much as it appears to dissolve to make it fluffy and spongelike. So you stir the vinegar in very slowly. You must not stir it fast. You have to kind of gum it around a little bit, skim over it, until it catches up, and then mix it very slowly. Then, after it gets caught and begins to get spongy, you can stir it faster and faster and faster.

Then, after the vinegar, you put in Worcestershire sauce. I should say you would put in about a tablespoonful and a half; but again, as in the other instance, you put in what appears to be necessary to make it fluffy and spongelike, and of a consistency that appears proper to the sensible discretion of one who is educated in the culinary art. [Laughter.]

After that has been slowly stirred, and then stirred a little faster, you take strained lemon juice, and you put in about, I should say, three tea- spoonsful of lemon juice. That thins it out a good deal. You stir it very fast from the start, so that it does not become clabber-like, so that it retains its liquid consistency; and then, when you have stirred it with the lemon juice, you put in paprika pepper. For an ordinary person's taste, you put in enough pepper to give it a fairly good red color.

Mr. President, when you have stirred that up thoroughly, you have the genuine Roquefort cheese salad dressing. It should be eaten with lettuce only. Roquefort cheese salad dressing should be eaten with head lettuce only. About a quarter and a half a quarter of a head of lettuce is about the proper portion for one person.

Mr. McCARRAN. Mr. President—

The PRESIDING OFFICER (Mr. CLARK in the chair). Does the Senator from Louisiana yield to the Senator from Nevada?

Mr. LONG. I yield to the Senator from Nevada.

Mr. McCARRAN. I inquire of the Senator from Louisiana what his recipe has to do with the recent declaration of the Executive as to the distribu- tion of wealth through taxation?

—Sens. Huey P. Long (D-La.) and Pat McCarran (D-Nev.)
June 13, 1935

THE BEST COFFEE ON EARTH

Mr. MILLS. Mr. Speaker, I ask unanimous consent for the immediate consideration of the bill (H.R. 9308) to extend for 3 years the suspension of duty on imports of crude chicory and the reduction in duty on ground chicory....

Mr. HAYS. Mr. Speaker, will the gentleman yield that I may ask the gentleman from Louisiana a question?

Mr. MILLS. I yield.

Mr. HAYS. There is no shortage of coffee now, is there?

Mr. BOGGS. As a matter of fact, I understand there is an oversupply.

Mr. HAYS. So if this bill were defeated would it be possible to get a cup of coffee in New Orleans?

Mr. BOGGS. Yes; but not as good as coffee with chicory. That, of course, is the best coffee on earth.

Mr. HAYS. There is a difference of opinion about that.

Mr. BOGGS. I admitted that there is a difference, but the gentleman understands that is the best coffee on earth.

Mr. HOFFMAN of Michigan. I understood the gentleman to say this is an additive to coffee.

Mr. BOGGS. That may not be the proper word.

Mr. HOFFMAN. The gentleman meant an adulteration.

Mr. BOGGS. Oh, no. It improves the coffee. It makes it delicious. We prefer our coffee as strong as love, as black as sin, and as hot as Hades.

> —*Reps. Wilbur D. Mills (D-Ark.), Wayne L. Hays (D-Ohio),*
> *T. Hale Boggs (D-La.), and Clare E. Hoffman (R-Mich.)*
> *March 2, 1960*

CAVEAT EMPTOR

Mr. BEALL. Mr. President, I rise to defend the fair name of the great Free State of Maryland against an insult.

Just as the distinguished Senators from Georgia would resent a knotty little peach being called "a Georgia peach," just as the Senators from Idaho would resent a puny little spud being called "an Idaho potato," just as the distinguished Senators from Maine would resent a crawfish being called "a Maine lobster," and just as the distinguished Senators from Kentucky would resent cheap bootleg being called "Kentucky bourbon" I resent the crabcakes being served in the Senate dining room being called "Maryland crabcakes."

On the menu, it says, bold and brazen, "Maryland crabcakes," but no Marylander would recognize what is served. Now, I do not say that the crabcakes served in the Senate dining room are bad; I simply say they fall far short of the high standard of "Maryland crabcakes," that tasty dish which has helped to make the name "Maryland" loved throughout the Nation.

Patrons of our dining room should be protected from deception.

I want the world to know that those crabcakes are not "Maryland crabcakes."

Mr. HILL. I may say to the Senator that we would like to have a demonstration of the superiority of Maryland crabcakes to those served in the Senate dining room.

Mr. BEALL. I promise the Senator from Alabama that that will be done.

—Sens. James G. Beall (R-Md.) and Joseph L. Hill (D-Ala.)
January 18, 1963

CAN'T BE BEAT

Mr. MATHIAS. Mr. President, one of the great cultural contributions of Maryland to the culinary arts is the beaten biscuit, one of the great favorites of the present occupant of the Chair. Today we are fortunate to be able to enjoy beaten biscuits baked by Ruth Orrell, one of Maryland's preeminent culinary artists for over 50 years.

I have traveled to the Eastern Shore more times than I can count to obtain these unique biscuits—so distinctive with their crunchy exterior and soft, doughy interior. And I have served them to guests both from inside of Maryland and outside, to Americans and people who visit us from abroad. They all agree that Mrs. Orrell's beaten biscuits are like no others, any place in the world.

I have a suggestion to make to Senators who will serve in the Senate in the 100th Congress. I strongly recommend that they add Maryland beaten biscuits to the menu in the Senate dining room. Beaten biscuits would be an appropriate indigenous, as well as a delicious, addition to the gustatory opportunities available to those who dine under the Capitol dome....

Mr. SIMPSON. Mr. President, it is just a curious set of circumstances as I came in to hear the Senator from Maryland speaking about the Maryland beaten biscuits because I, when I was practicing law in Cody, WY, used to read the CONGRESSIONAL RECORD and I saw this remarkable tribute to these peculiar—I mean this particular food item, and I have tried them since then. Senator MATHIAS has shared these with me, and they are like eating agates. They are very, very hard and difficult, but they are very good. I say to the Senator as he leaves this body, not only has he shared with me the mysteries of beaten biscuits, he has taught me about deciduous trees and shared with me a great deal of his extraordinary warmth and humanity and this Senator will miss him greatly.

—Sens. Charles McC. Mathias, Jr. (R-Md.) and Alan K. Simpson (R-Wyo.)
October 17, 1986

SHELL GAMES

Mr. AuCOIN. Mr. Speaker, I am so glad the Louisiana delegation is here this morning, and I want them to listen very carefully to my remarks.

Mr. Speaker, it's been 181 years since Meriwether Lewis and William Clark set out from the Louisiana Territory in search of a delicacy superior to anything they ever tasted there.

It has been documented that Lewis and Clark had a tremendous craving for crawfish. One day, after polishing off a bucket of boiled Louisiana mud bugs, as they were called then, Lewis turned to Clark and said, "Bill, is this as good as it gets?"

The rest, of course, is history. When they reached Oregon, Lewis and Clark's arduous search for the perfect crawfish was finally rewarded.

Ever since, Mr. Speaker, the succulent delicacy which we in Oregon know as the evergreen lobster has been one of my State's most guarded treasures, available only to Oregonians.

Tomorrow in New Orleans, a selected number of Louisiana crawfish lovers will be given a taste of what they've been missing all these years. We do not do this out of cruelty, Mr. Speaker, but only to settle a friendly dispute between our two States over whose crawfish should be crowned king.

Representing Oregon in the Crawfish Culinary Cup competition will be our own great chef, Marcel Lahsene of Jake's Famous Crawfish Restaurant in Portland. He has prepared two new dishes, "Crawfish Monique," and "Crawfish McCall," the latter named after the late Oregon Governor, Tom McCall.

I have no doubt that any objective comparison will establish the clear superiority of Oregon's wild and winsome crawfish over its tame and timid Louisiana cousin.

Mr. FRANK. Mr. Speaker, will the gentleman yield?

Mr. AuCOIN. I yield to the gentleman from Massachusetts.

PARLIAMENTARY INQUIRY

Mr. FRANK. Mr. Speaker, I would like to propound a parliamentary inquiry.

The SPEAKER pro tempore. The gentleman will state his parliamentary inquiry.

Mr. FRANK. Mr. Speaker, there has been a lot of concern on the other side about the rules. I know we all want to abide by them. We have been warned against speaking ill of the other body or speaking ill of the President. I want to make sure there is nothing in the rules that says that you cannot cast aspersions on Louisiana crawfish.

Mr. AuCOIN. Absolutely. I checked the rules completely. The Louisiana mud bug does not qualify.

Mr. FRANK. I thank the chair.

Mr. ROEMER. Mr. Speaker, I do not care what AuCOIN says; everybody knows that real crawfish come from Louisiana. Here comes AuCOIN this morning talking Oregon crawfish; you have got to be kidding me, LES.

Now, I know I am naive. When I first came to Congress I believed in supply side economics. KEMP had me convinced if we cut the marginal tax rate to zero the Treasury would be overflowing with money. I know I am naive.

When I first came to Congress I thought the House budget bill would actually lower the deficit. I know I am naive. When I first came to Congress I thought that the budget vote was an economic, not a political one. I know I am naive. But crawfish from Oregon?

Listen, LES, look at the Louisiana delegation: BREAUX knows crawfish; LIVINGSTON knows crawfish; TAUZIN knows crawfish; BOGGS knows crawfish; MOORE knows crawfish; ROEMER knows crawfish. But, LES, let me tell you, you might know plywood; but crawfish you know from nothing.

— Reps. Les AuCoin (D-Oreg.), Barney Frank (D-Mass.), and
Buddy Roemer (D-La.)
June 26, 1985

THE CHILI WARS: ROUND I

Mr. TOWER obtained the floor.

Mr. GOLDWATER. Mr. President, a parliamentary inquiry. Will the Senator from Texas use his microphone? If he is going to insult me, I want to hear it.

Mr. TOWER. Mr. President, I note from an article in the Houston Chronicle of this past weekend that the junior Senator from Arizona, the Honorable BARRY GOLDWATER, apparently made some comment on Texas chili at a function this past week at the National Press Club.

The Chronicle quoted the Arizona Senator as saying: "I have heard that the club serves only Texas chili. Tell me this is not true. A Texan does not know chili from leavings in a corral."

Now, Mr. President, if this is an accurate quote of the distinguished junior Senator from Arizona, I submit that this raises very grave questions about that Senator's taste.

The whole world knows, Mr. President, that the best chili anywhere is brewed in Texas. Ask any Texan over the age of 3 months if there are any doubts lingering in the mind of anyone. Is not Texas the site for the annual world's champion chili cookoff at Terlingua? Is Texas not the home of the late great chili king, Wick Fowler, whose family still packages the world-famous Two Alarm Chili at Austin? Is the Chili Appreciation Society International not headquartered at Dallas, where some of the world's foremost chili experts reside?

Comparing Arizona chili to Texas chili is like comparing Phyllis Diller to Sophia Loren.

Mr. President, every Texan who has ever cooked chili knows he could make better chili than anyone from Arizona with one hand tied behind his back.

The junior senator from Arizona has gone too far. A Texan just cannot take this lying down. I therefore, Mr. President, challenge the junior Senator from Arizona to a chili cookoff. The junior Senator from Arizona, if he chooses to accept this challenge, can choose the time and place for this chili cookoff with three impartial judges mutually agreed on. This will prove once again that nobody can cook chili like a Texan—not even Arizona's most distinguished citizen, who is grievously in error on this point.

Mr. GOLDWATER. Mr. President, the Senator from Texas still did not clear up the remark I made about not knowing chili from leavings in a corral.

Mr. TOWER. We know that an Arizonan cannot tell the difference.

Mr. GOLDWATER. But the Senator from Texas will not name that substance with which to make chili which they use a lot in Texas because they do not know the difference. [Laughter.]

Mr. ROBERT C. BYRD. Mr. President, may we have order in the Senate?

The PRESIDING OFFICER. The Senate will be in order.

Mr. GOLDWATER. Mr. President, I will be very glad to accept the challenge. It will be a real experience for me to teach a Texan how to do something that he does not know how to.

Mr. TOWER. Mr. President, that remains to be seen.

> —*Sens. John Tower (R-Tex.), Barry Goldwater (R-Ariz.), and*
> *Robert C. Byrd (D-W. Va.)*
> *February 5, 1974*

THE CHILI WARS: ROUND II

Mr. DOMENICI. Mr. President, great wars can sometimes develop from seemingly small conflicts. Thus the alleged cutting off of Captain Jenkins' ear by a Spanish guardacosta in 1739 ended in the War of the Austrian Succession involving every great power in Europe.

In the interests of preventing a civil war between the great and sovereign States of Texas and Arizona, over the quality of their respective chilies it would seem appropriate for New Mexico—acting in the finest traditions of international relations—to tender its good offices.

Both nature and man would seem to have dictated that New Mexico become the peacemaker. We sit between the two quasi-belligerents. Thus at present only geopolitical considerations prevent an actual invasion by Texas Chili Rangers in retaliation for the claims of the Arizona Chili Commandos.

But, even more important, the would-be peacemaker must grasp the basic causes of the conflict—must have a complete understanding of the underlying reasons for a casus belli—and bring that knowledge to bear in the peace negotiations.

Mr. President, the cause of this conflict between the two great States can be stated simply: they are brandishing soup ladles over the quality of the respective chilies for which both are justly famous.

Would that they could appeal to that "Great Chili Maker in the Sky" to settle their differences.

Unless and until His good offices are tendered, it would seem most fitting for the best chilimaker—and I refer in all due humility, of course, to New Mexico—to settle this quarrel.

New Mexico chili is so renowned, so superior, so smoothly saturated with the fiery elixirs of peppers that make great chili, as to be prized by chili aficionados the world over.

We do not boast—we need not advertise—for like a great estate wine produced in limited quantities, true connoisseurs know it, speak of it in awe, seek it eagerly, bid fantastic prices for it when we allow it to be purchased outside our borders.

In other words, New Mexico chili is numero uno—the winner of gold medals at gourmet festivals since the first Spanish explorers came to Nuevo Mexico in the 17th century.

Thus, the real issue is whether Arizona or Texas chili be designated as second best in the world—and who better can make this decision in a calm and judicious manner that the admittedly supreme masters of the cusine de la chili?

We can be muy simpatico to the eager hopes of these talented, but rather inexperienced practitioners of the chili art. We will judge solely by comparison with our chili, and whichever comes closest—admittedly neither can come too close—will receive our benign approval and be given the silver medal. The gold medal, of course, will always remain in the sacred confines of New Mexico.

Mr. President, we have made our offer—we can do no more but hope that this will avert war between two peoples now standing at "Chilies Point" with one another.

—Sen. Pete V. Domenici (R-N. Mex.)
February 7, 1974

THE CHILI WARS: ROUND III

Mr. TAFT. Mr. President, I could not fail to note certain remarks by the distinguished Senators from Texas and Arizona regarding the quality of their respective States' chili. Each likened the other chili to barnyard apples, and possibly both spoke truly. The point they missed is the secret of tenderness and tang by this standard. The only real chili comes from Cincinnati, Ohio.

Whereas southwestern chili, both in flavor and effect, guarantees new vires of Montezuma's revenge, Cincinnati chili draws on the subtleties of the Balkans for its spicing. In a recent test conducted by the chili institute, a blindfolded subject, upon tasting southwestern chili, reported "images of Texans mowing down helpless Mexicans and then ransacking their mess kits." Cincinnati chili, on the other hand, brought a detailed description of the floor plan of the Castle of Zenda. Needless to say, the desperate attempts of pseudo Latinos to cover the taint of fatigue bear little comparison with the cuisine of provinces trod by Lucullus and Vitellius.

I can promise my distinguished colleagues from Texas and Arizona that a Cincinnati three-way and a couple of cheese coneys at an Empress or Skyline chili parlor will deflate both their provincial egos and their lower tracts. Indeed, I think it symbolic that Cincinnati chili is served over spaghetti, but southwestern chili is accompanied by beans.

I ask unanimous consent that a full report on the superiorities of Cincinnati chili, prepared by one of the world's foremost chili cognoscente, be printed in the RECORD for the further enlightenment of my benighted colleagues....

—Sen. Robert Taft, Jr. (R-Ohio)
February 7, 1974

THE CHILI WARS: ROUND IV

Mr. MONTOYA. Mr. President, I have noted with interest and some amusement the "chili" war which seems to have been touched off at that famous Mexican restaurant, "The National Press Club," between two distinguished U.S. Senators from the States of Arizona and Texas.

When my fellow Senator from New Mexico, PETE DOMENICI, offered to settle the dispute by selecting the world's second best chili in a chili competition between the two bellicose chili-loving States, I applauded his diplomatic gesture and wished him well as a peacemaker.

However, recent events have forced me to speak out. The war of the chili has now spread to other States, with the Senator from Ohio (Mr. TAFT) and the Senator from Oklahoma (Mr. BELLMON) challenging the others for second place. I felt that I am perhaps in the best position to mediate and bring peace with honor back to the U.S. Senate and the National Press Club. It is certainly no time for further brushfire wars, over hot chilies, either red or green....

In order to clarify the position of the chili in the history of this continent and to speed a better understanding of the negotiations which I am prepared to pursue as mediator, I have requested that the publication "Chile" be sent from the New Mexico State University Cooperative Extension Service to all Senators, and that several copies be made available to the National Press Club for use by investigative reporters who wish to properly cover hot stories and raise national steam levels.

In addition to the more formal history of the "Chile" pamphlet, I will also send copies of "Della Montoya's Famous Recipes," a publication much sought after by those who know their chili facts.

I hope, Mr. President, that my remarks will be accepted in their spirit of friendship and multicultural understanding.

Mr. ERVIN. Mr. President, will the Senator yield?

Mr. MONTOYA. I yield.

Mr. ERVIN. Mr. President, I merely want to say that the eloquent statement about chili, by the distinguished senior Senator from New Mexico, has convinced the Senator from North Carolina that his is the next best dish to North Carolina barbeque.

—Sens. Joseph M. Montoya (D-N. Mex.) and Sam J. Ervin, Jr. (D-N.C.)
February 19, 1974

*Cloture
Ex Mero Muto
and Other
Parliamentary
Mumbo-Jumbo*

OYEZ!
OYEZ!
OYEZ!

PARLEZ-VOUS SENATE?

THE VICE PRESIDENT. The Senator is correct.

Mr. ALLEN. A mere motion could not say that it is not going to be debatable; it would not have any effect until it has been ratified by a vote of the Senate, would it?

THE VICE PRESIDENT. The second and third parts of that motion would have to be put immediately to the Senate for the vote.

Mr. ALLEN. And the Senate—is the Chair going to invoke cloture ex mero motu?

Is the Chair going to invoke cloture on his own motion?

THE VICE PRESIDENT. Will the Senator put that in English for me?

[Laughter.]

—*Vice President Nelson A. Rockefeller (R-N.Y.) and Sen. James B. Allen (D-Ala.)*
March 1, 1975

THE SITUATION

Mr. CHAFEE. Mr. President, I am deeply disturbed over what I understand took place here last Saturday. If someone can tell me I am wrong, I will be glad to hear it. As I understand the situation, the claim is now made that a vote on germaneness before cloture and after cloture is exactly the same matter. So that when we are in a situation when cloture is invoked, and someone comes along with a totally nongermane amendment, the Chair rules it as nongermane, the appeal is taken to the ruling of the Chair, 51 Senators vote that it is germane, the matter then comes up for consideration, and because cloture has been invoked, the matter no longer can be debated beyond the postcloture limit of 100 hours and 51 Senators can go on and approve it.

That is the situation. No one has yet disputed to me that it is, and if it is, we are really in an extraordinarily different situation than any of us have known previously.

If that is indeed the situation ...

—Sen. John H. Chafee (R-R.I.)
October 1, 1984

A SUBSTITUTE FOR THE SUBSTITUTE FOR THE SUBSTITUTE

Mr. ROBERT C. BYRD. At the present time there is not any agreement on that point.

Mr. President, may I inquire of the Chair as to what is the nature of Mr. KENNEDY'S amendment?

The PRESIDING OFFICER. This is a substitute for the substitute for the substitute.

[Laughter.]

Mr. ROBERT C. BYRD. Mr. President, a further parliamentary inquiry.

The PRESIDING OFFICER. The Senator will state it.

Mr. ROBERT C. BYRD. Is the amendment that has just been offered by Mr. KENNEDY the Pearson-Bentsen language?

Mr. KENNEDY. The answer to that question is no.

The PRESIDING OFFICER. No, it is not.

Mr. BUMPERS. Mr. President, will the Senator from Massachusetts yield for a parliamentary inquiry?

Mr. KENNEDY. Yes.

The PRESIDING OFFICER. The Senator will state it.

Mr. BUMPERS. So we will all know what we are doing here, first, is the amendment of the Senator from Washington in the nature of a substitute for Pearson-Bentsen?

Mr. JACKSON. The Senator is correct.

Mr. BUMPERS. Then the Pearson-Bentsen amendment was a substitute for the bill, the amendment of the Senator from Washington is a substitute for the Pearson-Bentsen amendment, and would it not then be the case that only perfecting amendments to the amendment of the Senator from Washington would be in order?

Mr. JACKSON. The Chair will have to answer that, but I would say the answer is no.

The PRESIDING OFFICER. At this point, the amendment of the Senator from Washington is amendable in one degree. The amendment of the Senator from Kansas and the Senator from Texas is amendable in two degrees, and the bill itself is amendable in two degrees.

It should have been stated in the reverse order from that in which the Chair just stated it.

Mr. BUMPERS. I certainly appreciate the clarification.

[Laughter.]

Mr. ROBERT C. BYRD. One further parliamentary inquiry, Mr. President.

The PRESIDING OFFICER. The Senator will state it.

Mr. ROBERT C. BYRD. I believe I am correct in saying, in order that the whole picture may be complete, that the amendment by Mr. KENNEDY is not open to amendment.

The PRESIDING OFFICER. That is correct.

Mr. BUMPERS. A further parliamentary inquiry.

The PRESIDING OFFICER. The Senator will state it.

Mr. BUMPERS. As I understand it, the Pearson-Bentsen amendment is a substitute for the bill. Is that correct?

The PRESIDING OFFICER. That is correct.

Mr. BUMPERS. The Jackson amendment is a substitute for Pearson-Bentsen?

The PRESIDING OFFICER. That is correct.

Mr. BUMPERS. And the Kennedy amendment is a substitute for Jackson?

The PRESIDING OFFICER. That is also correct.

Mr. BUMPERS. And we are not down to a third-degree amendment?

The PRESIDING OFFICER. Under the precedents of the Senate, the first full substitute for the bill does not kill a degree. It is a freebie.

[Laughter.]

> — *Sens. Robert C. Byrd (D-W. Va.), Edward Zorinsky (D-Nebr.)(Presiding Officer), Dale Bumpers (D-Ark.), Edward M. Kennedy (D-Mass.), and Henry M. Jackson (D-Wash.)*
> *September 23, 1977*

CRUEL AND UNUSUAL PUNISHMENT

Mr. KASTENMEIER. Mr. Speaker, I ask unanimous consent that it shall be in order to consider in the House, any rule of the House to the contrary notwithstanding, a motion to take from the Speaker's table the bill (H.R. 5479) to amend section 504 of title 5, United States Code, and section 2412 of title 28, United States Code, with respect to awards of expenses of certain agency and court proceedings, and for other purposes, with a Senate amendment to the House amendment to the Senate amendments thereto, and to concur in the Senate amendment to the House amendment to the Senate amendments with an amendment, and that the previous question be considered as ordered on the motion.

The SPEAKER pro tempore. Is there objection to the request of the gentleman from Wisconsin?

— Rep. Robert W. Kastenmeier (D-Wis.)
October 4, 1984

SOMEWHERE ALONG THE LINE I HAD AN AMENDMENT

Mr. FUQUA. Mr. Chairman, I have a parliamentary inquiry.

The CHAIRMAN pro tempore. The Chair will advise the Members that there is a reasonably complex situation before the Committee. To attempt to elucidate it, we must have order. The Chair will advise the gentleman from Florida the order in which the questions will be put.

The gentleman from Florida (Mr. FUQUA) will state his parliamentary inquiry.

Mr. FUQUA. Mr. Chairman, prior to the recent vote there was an amendment offered by the gentleman from Pennsylvania (Mr. KOSTMAYER) to the amendment offered by the gentleman from Washington (Mr. McCORMACK) as a substitute for the amendment offered by the gentleman from Pennsylvania (Mr. KOSTMAYER), as modified. Somewhere along the line I had an amendment to the Kostmayer amendment. Could the Chair state the parliamentary situation and the sequence in which the votes will occur?

The CHAIRMAN pro tempore. The Chair will attempt to do so. The Chair will inform the Committee that all time has expired. The order in which the votes will be put is as follows: The first vote will occur on the amendment offered by the gentleman from Florida (Mr. FUQUA) to the amendment offered by the gentleman from Pennsylvania (Mr. KOSTMAYER), as modified. The second vote will occur on the amendment offered by the gentleman from Pennsylvania (Mr. KOSTMAYER) to the amendment offered by the gentleman from Washington (Mr. McCORMACK) as a substitute for the amendment offered by the gentleman from Pennsylvania (Mr. KOSTMAYER), as modified. The third vote will occur on the amendment offered by the gentleman from Washington (Mr. McCORMACK) as a substitute for the amendment offered by the gentleman from Pennsylvania (Mr. KOSTMAYER), as modified and the final vote will be on the original Kostmayer amendment as amended. The Chair will now put the question.

The question is on the amendment offered by the gentleman from Florida (Mr. FUQUA) to the amendment offered by the gentleman from Pennsylvania (Mr. KOSTMAYER), as modified.

The amendment to the amendment, as modified, was agreed to.

The CHAIRMAN pro tempore. The question is on the amendment offered by the gentleman from Pennsylvania (Mr. KOSTMAYER), as modified, to the amendment offered by the gentleman from Washington (Mr. McCORMACK) as a substitute for the amendment offered by the gentleman from Pennsylvania (Mr. KOSTMAYER), as modified, as amended.

The question was taken; and the Chairman announced that the noes appeared to have it.

—Reps. Don Fuqua (D-Fla.) and Gerry E. Studds (D-Mass.) (Presiding Officer)
October 18, 1979

AMENDMENT IN THE SECOND DEGREE

Mr. MOYNIHAN. I thank the chair.

Mr. President, the distinguished Senator from New Hampshire is on the floor. Am I correct that this Xerox copy is the amendment to the Budget Act that we are going to act on today? It says "to committee, as modified." Has this gone to the Finance Committee?

Mr. RUDMAN. I believe I understand the question of the Senator from New York. The modification refers to the modification offered by the Senator from Pennsylvania to an amendment which I think bears the name of a Senator from New York which was the committee amendment pending. This is offered as a second-degree amendment to that amendment as modified.

Mr. MOYNIHAN. Am I to take it that this could end up as the Moynihan-Gramm-Rudman-Hollings amendment?

Mr. RUDMAN. We certainly hope so. [Laughter.]

Mr. MOYNIHAN. Mr. President, I urgently suggest the absence of a quorum. [Laughter.]

The PRESIDING OFFICER. The clerk will urgently call the roll.

—Sens. Daniel Patrick Moynihan (D-N.Y.) and Warren Rudman (R-N.H.)
July 23, 1983

ROLL CALL

The PRESIDING OFFICER. A quorum is present.

Mr. ROBERT C. BYRD. Vote.

The PRESIDING OFFICER. The question is on agreeing to the motion to lay on the table the motion to reconsider the vote by which the motion to lay on the table the motion to proceed to the consideration of the fair housing bill was rejected.

On this question, the yeas and nays have been ordered, and the clerk will call the roll.

The legislative clerk called the roll....

The result was announced—yeas 61, nays 31...

So the motion to lay on the table the motion to reconsider the vote by which the motion to lay on the table the motion to proceed to the consideration of the fair housing bill (H.R. 5200) was rejected was agreed to.

—December 4, 1980

PREPOSITION PROPOSITION

Mr. BUMPERS. Mr. President, I always wonder what my English teacher thinks when she hears me say, "I ask unanimous consent that further reading be dispensed with," because I was taught that one absolute "no-no" in English is never to end a sentence with a preposition. So I just trust she will forgive me one of the little indiscretions that is demanded by the great deliberative body.

Incidentally, you remember Winston Churchill said, "Ending a sentence with a preposition is something up with which I will not put."

—Sen. Dale Bumpers (D-Ark.)
February 1, 1984

**CHAMBER
MUSIC**

*You have done
dinner theater, David,
have you not?*

CHAMBER
MUSIC

YOU HAVE DONE DINNER THEATER, DAVID, HAVE YOU NOT?

Mr. DREIER of California. I also thought that I would take a few moments to talk about another classmate of mine, GENE CHAPPIE. GENE prides himself on being a person who speaks his mind. GENE has often been labeled irreverent and he refuses to deny that label.

He sent a letter to several of us just recently, and I would like to share that letter with the House, Mr. Speaker.

This one says: "Dear David, as the monkey said when his tail got caught in the lawn mower, it won't be long now. With the days running out for this short-timer, I wanted to take a minute to thank you for your counsel, friendship and support on those issues of importance to northern California."

He goes on to talk about what a privilege it was to serve with us. He said, "Will Rogers once said there is no trick to being a humorist when you have the whole Government working for you."

With that in mind, he, and I assume a member of his staff, put together a rendition of the tune "My Favorite Things," which we all remember very well from "The Sound of Music."

I would like to yield for a comment specifically on that to my distinguished colleague, the gentleman from California [Mr. DORNAN].

Mr. DORNAN of California. Thanks awfully, David.

These three honored people are in the gallery enjoying every precious moment, every treasured word. They are not here.

Mr. DREIER of California. We are not to refer to the gallery.

Mr. DORNAN of California. Oh, they are watching from their offices, bless their little hearts.

Mr. DREIER of California. But we are not to address them in their offices, based on House rules.

Mr. DORNAN of California. That is right; there is no television here. I keep forgetting.

Mr. DREIER of California. That is right.

Mr. DORNAN of California. Reality keeps impinging upon the truth, as we know it in the House.

I am ready, David.

Mr. DREIER of California. This is called GENE CHAPPIE's ode to Congress, or these are a few of the funniest things.

Mr. DORNAN of California. Do we sing? Again, a violation of House rules.

Mr. DREIER of California. Mr. Speaker—

Mr. DORNAN of California. Yes, we would never even think of singing. Mr. Speaker, forget the mere mention of it.

Mr. DREIER of California. Mr. Speaker, is it a violation of House rules to sing on the House floor?

The SPEAKER pro tempore. If the gentlemen wish to do so, the Chair will not infringe upon the vocal attributes of the gentlemen from California.

Mr. DORNAN of California. You have caved in too easily, Mr. Speaker. I thought you would save us from this temptation. Maybe a Richard-Burton-in-Camelot compromise, sort of talk singing. You have done dinner theater, DAVID, have you not?

Mr. DREIER of California. No.

Mr. DORNAN of California. My distinguished colleague from Pomona.

Mr. DREIER of California. I would like to yield to the gentleman from Fresno.

Mr. PASHAYAN. Thank you very much. I wish I could stay to join the chorus here, but if I might be given a minute of solo—

Mr. DORNAN of California. Your voice is tightening up, I understand. If you sing, you will lose for sure.

Mr. PASHAYAN. I understand that, but I want to point out simply the unusual proportion of the Members that we are unfortunately losing from the great State of California, one from the southern part and two from the northern. By the mathematics of the population that exists in the State and the proportions opportunate thereunto, it ought to be, of course, the reverse.

Mr. DORNAN of California. Oh, no. To the contrary, Mr. Northerner.

Mr. PASHAYAN. I am Mr. Central, thank you.

Mr. DORNAN of California. Right.

Mr. PASHAYAN. These three have—

Mr. DORNAN of California. You moderate.

Mr. MOORHEAD. I think our great Member from Orange County here, ROBERT DORNAN, has the most mellow voice and will be able to do the best job in leading us. ROBERT, why don't you go ahead.

Mr. DREIER of California. Having gotten permission to sing it—

Mr. DORNAN of California. I will lead off. We might get into this. I will lead off, asking the people to think of "These are a few of my favorite things." So this is the melody to the tune of "My Favorite Things," a poem, stolen musically, but written, the book, as we say on Broadway, the lyrics, written in the manner of Rodgers and Hammerstein, by GENE CHAPPIE.

Wait a minute, we cannot go together or they will never hear it.

Mr. DREIER of California. No, no, we are singing this together.

Mr. DORNAN of California. I am 20 years older than you; I will go first and you will take the second one. DUNCAN, you take the third one.

Tuesdays through Thursdays, and half-hour sessions.
Rollcalls and quorums, and eighty suspensions.
Boll Weevils, Young Turks, right and left wings.
These are a few of the funniest things.

When the bell rings,
When the whip calls,
When I'm on the floor,
I simply remember the funniest things, and wonder why I ask for more.

Lawyers and lobbyists and those who want money.
Balancing the budget, Isn't that funny?
National Brick Week, This and that day.
Can anyone think of a better way?

When the letters come,
When the press calls,
When there are meetings all day.
I simply remember the funniest things, and tomorrow may bring what it may.

Presidents and Secretaries, urge your support.
Flying the red eye, to get back and forth.
Constituents who need help, Bureaucrats who won't.
For those seeking office, my advice is "Don't."

When the money's gone,
When the government closes,
When the CR fails
I'll pack my bags, let the phone ring, and always remember the funniest things.

As GENO fades into the distance in his camper, stealing one old Henny Youngman joke after another, I say, as the Sun sets in the high Sierras, fond adieu, GENO, you Italian-American happy guy, you brought us hours and hours of riotous laughter in the House.

—Reps. David Dreier (R-Calif.), Robert K. Dornan (R-Calif.), Charles Pashayan, Jr. (R-Calif.), and Carlos J. Moorhead (R-Calif.)
October 16, 1986

QUEEN OF HAWAIIAN ENTERTAINERS

Mr. MATSUNAGA. Mr. Speaker, it is difficult to know where to begin in praising the accomplishments of a genuinely sincere and vibrant human being like Hilo Hattie. Her past 70 years of singing and dancing to cheer up the human race has left an endearing sense of warmth, well-being and aloha in the hearts of the people of Hawaii and all those who have come to know her as an entertainer and beloved Kamaaina. She made songs such as "Manuela Boy," "The Cockeyed Mayor of Kaunakakai," and "Becky, I Ain't Coming Home No More" famous in her inimitable down-to-earth style....

—Sen. Spark M. Matsunaga (D-Hawaii)
August 21, 1974

NEW JERSEY TO THEE

Mr. PATTEN. Mr. Speaker, one of my talented constituents, Mrs. Marie L. Chiasson, of Morgan, N.J., has written the words and music to a song I like, "New Jersey To Thee." Its popularity is growing all the time.

New Jersey is a fine State, but it is hard to express the feelings our people have for it. However, I believe that Marie Chiasson has succeeded in describing those proud feelings, so I am inserting the words in the CONGRESSIONAL RECORD in order that my colleagues will know more about the attributes of New Jersey—a small, but outstanding State:

NEW JERSEY TO THEE
(Music and Lyrics by Marie L. Chiasson)

It's a state to be proud of the state of New Jersey,
Founded in sixteen sixty four
Made famous in history, her heroes are many and Washington fought for her shores.

To thee. To thee. New Jersey, New Jersey to thee,
There's many a story that's told of her glory, one state of the land which is free,
We'll progress together for ever and ever,
New Jersey, New Jersey to thee!

CHORUS

To thee. To thee. New Jersey, New Jersey to thee,
With love for one another,
We'll share with our brother,
And help keep America Free.

— Rep. Edward J. Patten (D-N.J.)
February 19, 1975

A NONPARTISAN VIOLIN

Mr. ROBERT C. BYRD. Now, I would not anticipate the Senate being in session beyond the hour of 6 o'clock tomorrow evening for the same very wholesome reason that it was not in session beyond that hour one day last week, Thursday. Upon that occasion our friends across the aisle had a very delightful evening with delectable food and lots of fun, nourishment, and music and, I suppose, no dancing?

Mr. STEVENS. We danced.

Mr. ROBERT C. BYRD. You danced. So the friends of mine on this side of the aisle are going to have something along the same lines tomorrow night. Some people refer to it as a shindig. It is said that I may be asked to play a tune or two on my violin. I do not know why I was not asked to attend last Thursday's function to play my violin. It is a nonpartisan violin. It knows no political party. It plays just as well for Republican ears as it does for Democratic hearts, and I am not complaining. It is merely an observation that I wish to indulge in at this moment.

I see my distinguished friend, the very able minority leader, who has drawn his sword and is prepared to parry my thrust and is already mounting his faithful steed, and is getting ready for the charge, so I yield.

Mr. BAKER. Mr. President, I would not for one moment joust with the majority leader, especially on a matter on which he is so accomplished, and that is the rendition of musical selections in public.

I must say that the Republicans have much going for them, and they had a successful and delightful evening, and in no way can we hope to compete with the musical selections of the majority leader.

I must observe, however, the last time I watched the majority leader play in public some of the front row broke out in tears, and I commented later they must have been moved by the eloquence of his presentation. He said no, they were moved because they were musicians.

[Laughter.]

> *—Sens. Robert C. Byrd (D-W. Va.), Ted Stevens (R-Alaska), and*
> *Howard H. Baker, Jr. (R-Tenn.)*
> *May 24, 1977*

POTATO, GRENADA

Mr. SHANNON. Mr. Speaker, some 40 years ago, George Gershwin popularized a little ditty that went like this:

You like po-ta-to and I like po-tah-to,
You like to-ma-to, and I like to-mah-to,
Po-ta-to, po-tah-to, To-ma-to, to-mah-to!
Let's call the whole thing off!

At about the same time that Mr. Gershwin was writing his tune, Mr. Reagan was starring in the kind of movies that recent incidents in Grenada cannot help but remind one of. Think about it for a moment—a small Caribbean island, a band of bearded local militia, a lot of beautiful and confused residents, and throw in a few angry tourists for comic relief. Unfortunately, this is not a grade B movie, it is not even a very good script—two American marines have already lost their lives.

But if that is the way Mr. Reagan persists in looking at these issues, maybe he will listen to a little advice from Mr. Gershwin. If Gershwin were alive today, perhaps he would consider this rewrite:

You like po-ta-to, I like po-tah-to,
You say Gre-na-da, I say Gre-nah-da,
Po-ta-to, po-tah-to, Gre-na-da, Gre-nah-da,
Let's call the whole thing off.

— Rep. James M. Shannon (D-Mass.)
October 26, 1983

DEPARTMENT
OF
CORRECTIONS

Mistakes, after all,
are inevitable

DEPARTMENT
OF
CORRECTIONS

BOTH SIDES AGAINST THE MIDDLE

Mr. BAKER. Mr. President, I get tons of mail. At the office, at my house, even in my car. Most of it is from constituents and friends; the rest of it is usually junk mail. All the envelopes are addressed to "HOWARD H. BAKER, JR.": Magazine subscription offers for fabulous prizes, free money-saving coupons, and bills for credit cards I do not even have.

When a man who claims that he went to school with a person he describes as "my second cousin twice removed," writes to me for a White House appointment, he addresses the letter to HOWARD H. BAKER.

When my face appears on the TV, a little tag comes on the screen, Senator HOWARD H. BAKER.

Since I have arrived in this Chamber, the Senate has been in session for 2,597 days. I would guess that my name has appeared in the CONGRESSIONAL RECORD literally thousands of times.

Anyway, I have just received a copy of the year-end report of the Senate and the cover says that it was submitted by "the Honorable Howard N. Baker." Who is this Howard N. Baker, and why is he writing about the U.S. Senate? I firmly believe that we should have had a Member of the Senate write the report. However, this Baker has done a remarkable job with the report, and if I could find him I would personally shake his hand.

But seriously, in this age of cutbacks and savings to the Government, we may be at the stage where we should start cutting back as close to home as possible. I propose we do away with middle initials. I have not calculated the potential savings, but it could be significant. After all, who ever heard of Ronald W. Reagan, Bing L. Crosby, and Luke J. Skywalker?

Let us look on the bright side: If we do not use a middle initial, they cannot get it wrong.

—*Sen. Howard H. Baker, Jr. (R-Tenn.)*
January 28, 1982

EXPLETIVE DELETED

Mr. BAUCUS. Mr. President, yesterday I introduced the Family Farm Preservation Act and submitted for the RECORD several articles discussing the problem of pension fund investments in agricultural land.

By mistake, the printer included an unrelated article which followed the pension fund article I was highlighting in the Great Falls Tribune. The article entitled, "Obscenity Charge Filed Against Clerk" should not have been printed. I regret the misunderstanding, and I ask that the permanent RECORD be corrected.

The PRESIDING OFFICER. The permanent RECORD will be so corrected.

—*Sen. Max Baucus (D-Mont.)*
November 21, 1980

NO LADY IN THE HOUSE

Mr. BAUCUS. I will not burden the Senate with going down the entire list, but every State on the Senator's list is in the same category.

Finally, Madam President, one more point.

The PRESIDING OFFICER (Mr. GORTON). The Senator is informed that there is no longer a Madam President in the chair.

Mr. BAUCUS. The Senator thanks the Chair. The Senator is so wrapped up in this argument he did not notice the change in Presiding Officers.

—*Sen. Max Baucus (D-Mont.) and Slade Gorton (R-Wash.) (Presiding Officer)*
October 31, 1983

MISTAKES ARE INEVITABLE AND IRREVERSIBLE

Said Thomas Jefferson, with compelling eloquence:

Mistakes are inevitable and irreversible.

—*Sen. Philip A. Hart (D-Mich.)*
July 25, 1966

ANOTHER JANUARY 28

Mr. BAKER. Mr. President, I have just finished reading today's CON-GRESSIONAL RECORD, and I want to first express my pleasure at the un-seasonably warm and beautiful weather we are having on this January 28. Why, it feels like July outside. In fact, the weather is so nice, it makes me feel 6 months younger.

But come to think of it, there must be a mistake somewhere, because I have another CONGRESSIONAL RECORD with "January 28, 1982" printed on it. In fact, there is even a statement in the RECORD that I made on the floor that day about a "Year-End Report" by a Howard N. Baker. I am HOWARD H. BAKER, and I would still love to meet this man who I no doubt have so much in common with. He must exist someplace, because as we all know, the Government Printing Office does not make any mistakes.

Anyway, I want to take this opportunity to share with my colleagues a hobby of mine that I have kept to myself in the past, but now want to make public. I just love to predict things. Events, careers, whatever. And I want to make some of my more confident predictions on the floor this morning.

Since this is the end of January, we have some very big sporting events coming up, and I want to courageously declare that the New York Islanders will win the Stanley Cup, the Los Angeles Lakers will win the NBA Championship, and that, you will not believe this, Jimmy Connors will knock off John McEnroe and win Wimbledon. I know that these predictions are risky, but I am willing to speak out on the record. In addition, I believe that Prince Charles and Princess Diana will have a boy, and name it William, and that the Space Shuttle will have a series of dramatic successes.

On a more serious front, I see troubled waters. Waters leading to lands, islands. I see islands in trouble. Not in North America, though. Further south. In the South Atlantic. I think, the Falkland Islands. Yes, that is it, the Falkland Islands. I see trouble there real soon, and I am going to call Foreign Relations Committee Chairman PERCY today to notify him of my concerns.

I have other predictions, but I will not take up the Senate's time at this point. I think I will just go outside and enjoy the Sun before it gets colder. The GPO is predicting snow tonight.

—Sen. Howard H. Baker, Jr. (R-Tenn.)
July 29, 1982

OTHERWISE CORRECT

Mrs. SMITH of Maine. Madam President, a public official—and particularly Members of Congress—must expect all kinds of attacks, from serious to petty, from justified to unjustified, from sincere to contrived, from accurate to false.

I, myself, have been the target of many attacks and have become somewhat accustomed to them. However, I think probably the most petty, unjustified, contrived, and false attack ever made on me by a newspaper was that on the front page of the March 28, 1962, issue of Roll Call.

Within the short space of 16 lines in one column that publication managed to make 8 very specific falsehoods against me. For those who read the snide article, I would make the following corrections:

First. My stolen TV set was not a color set—it was a black and white set.

Second. It was not an expensive set.

Third. It was not stolen in broad daylight but instead, during the night, as I did not leave the office until after sunset that day.

Fourth. It was not stolen on the day of the Glenn orbit.

Fifth. I did not go into orbit.

Sixth. I did not taunt the Sergeant at Arms.

Seventh. I did not look into the police setup.

Eighth. I did not uncover Captain Harris, as I had never even heard of him until I read the story in the Washington Post....

—Sen. Margaret Chase Smith (R-Maine)
April 2, 1962

SITTING DOWN ON THE JOB

Mr. HECHLER of West Virginia. Mr. Speaker, having received unanimous consent to extend my remarks in the RECORD, I would like to indicate that I am really not speaking these words. Try as I might, I could not get the floor to deliver my plea on behalf of the coal miners disabled by pneumoconiosis. I do not want to kid anybody into thinking that I am now on my feet delivering a stirring oration. As a matter of fact, I am back in my office typing this out on my own hot little typewriter, far from the madding crowd, and somewhat removed from the House Chamber. Such is the pretense of the House that it would have been easy to just quietly include these remarks in the RECORD, issue a brave press release, and convince thousands of cheering constituents that I was in there fighting every step of the way, influencing the course of history in the heat of debate....

—Rep. Ken Hechler (D-W. Va.)
October 18, 1971

**THE
SPORTS
PAGE**

*If the Senator is going to
stay here and talk,
would he give me his
ticket to the Mets game?*

THE
SPORTS
PAGE

SHEA A LITTLE LONGER

Mr. DOMENICI. Will the Senator yield for a question without losing his right to the floor?

Mr. D'AMATO. Certainly.

Mr. DOMENICI. If the Senator is going to stay here and talk until Saturday night, would he give me his ticket to the Mets game? He can stay here and I will go.

—Sens. Pete V. Domenici (R-N. Mex.) and Alfonse M. D'Amato (R-N.Y.)
October 16, 1986

WANNA BET?

Mr. DORNAN of California. Mr. Speaker, I knew that it would eventually come to this. Your 50 years of glorious service, sir, riding on Fenway Park, and of all Members, who should have that beautiful stadium in Anaheim where the California Angels play, than this humble Member from California with 14 years of Federal service.

Mr. Speaker, I know what a good team the Pink Sox are. I know that when they face those Angels, there will be some in New England that think they will prevail. But you know, Mr. Speaker, going back to your catechism, as FREDDY ST GERMAIN knows, that the Seraphim, the Cherubim, the Thrones, the Dominations, the Virtues, the Powers, the Principalities, and the Archangels will be on the side of their ninth order of celestial glory, those who inhabit the beautiful Anaheim stadium.

Mr. ST GERMAIN. Mr. Speaker, will the gentleman yield?

Mr. DORNAN of California. I yield to the gentleman from Rhode Island.

Mr. ST GERMAIN. Let us make the record clear: It is the Red Sox. The Red Sox.

Mr. DORNAN of California. Excuse me, the Red Sox, sir. I stand corrected.

That pennant of the American League will not be flapping in some smoggy, fatty, wind breeze over in Boston. We know that when the final game is over, and it may not even reach seven, that the team that carries the name of an entire state, the glorious Angels of California, sir, will be the victors.

Therefore, I offer you the following friendly wager: I know the gentleman only bets in a gentlemanly way, but these are extraordinary circumstances. Four cases of the biggest, juiciest oranges in the history of mankind from the beautiful Orange County against one teeny, weeny, little lobster dinner, and you do not even have to be there to watch me eat it, sir.

One lobster dinner against four cases of oranges will be riding on the glory of the American League pennant. Good luck, Mr. Speaker, to you, the cradle of liberty, and all of New England, but that 40-knot breeze will be the orange-scented breezes of Orange County, CA, when victory is declared.

— *Reps. Robert K. Dornan (R-Calif.) and Fernand J. St Germain (D-R.I.)*
October 7, 1986

DISORDER IN THE HOUSE

H. RES. 429
IN THE HOUSE OF REPRESENTATIVES
February 16, 1927

Mr. GALLIVAN submitted the following resolution; which was referred to the Committee on Rules and ordered to be printed

RESOLUTION

Whereas the physical exercise of hostile encounter by means of human fists is becoming of daily occurrence in the House of Representatives; and

Whereas such encounters are being conducted in an irregular manner, with small regard to race, weight, reach, height, or classification of Members to insure quality and fair fighting; and

Whereas most of the principal communities of the United States have boxing boards or commissions, whose duty it is to regulate the sport and insure fair play: Therefore be it

Resolved, That a committee be appointed by the Speaker of the House, who shall be chairman ex officio, to be known as the Boxing Board of the House of Representatives, to have full authority in the arranging of bouts between Members according to weight, corporeal and mental, age, and experience; and be it further

Resolved, That said board shall arrange to hold the bouts in Statuary Hall, under the paternal eyes of the fathers of the Republic, and under no circumstances shall said board authorize bouts either in the House of Representatives or before committees of the House unless contestants sign written agreements, approved by the chairman, to abstain from hair pulling, profanity, and tobacco chewing, and the use of wrist watches or flasks; and be it further

Resolved, That the Honorable William D. Upshaw, of Georgia, is appointed permanent referee of all bouts held under the jurisdiction of said board, his salary and expenses to be paid out of the contingent fund of the House.

— Rep. James A. Gallivan (D-Mass.)
February 16, 1927

WHEN YOU ARE TEED OFF AT THE POST OFFICE REMEMBER LARRY RYAN

Mr. WILSON of California. Mr. Speaker, a recent item in the Washington Star told of one Larry Ryan who scored a hole-in-one while playing in the

Pittsfield, Mass., Post Office Golf Tournament. But his was a dubious achievement. He drove from the third tee and the ball went 180 yards away—into the cup on the first green.

Some would find this an apt analogy to the operations of the Postal Service. So, whenever you receive mail intended for another—a not uncommon occurrence—it is a safe guess that our Postal Service is using the Larry Ryan method of delivery.

—Rep. Charles H. Wilson (D-Calif.)
June 10, 1975

FOOTBALL REPORT

Mr. BUCHANAN. Mr. Speaker, I feel the time has come for me to give my colleagues a second report on the World Football League now that it is mid-season.

I am sure my colleagues will be interested to know that the Birmingham Americans now have a 10-0 record. This is only appropriate for an Alabama-based team, and one which represents the city which I must modestly admit is the finest in the United States.

We have put out the Chicago Fire. We have reduced the Florida Blaze to a dim glow. We have set the Southern California Sun. We have flattened the Detroit Wheels, and all those great achievements demonstrate that Americans can do anything when they try.

Mr. FREY. Mr. Speaker, will the gentleman yield?

Mr. BUCHANAN. I yield to the gentleman from Florida.

Mr. FREY. Mr. Speaker, I just wonder if the gentleman remembers the score of last year's Alabama-Notre Dame game.

Mr. BUCHANAN. I thank the gentleman very much for his contribution.

—Reps. John H. Buchanan, Jr. (R-Ala.) and Louis Frey, Jr. (R-Fla.)
September 11, 1974

SORE LOSER

Mr. BURTON of Indiana. Mr. Speaker, throughout this year I have been appalled at how the majority has stretched the rules of this House. I have continually tried to be quiet on this issue and have pledged to not attack any Member on this issue, but now, Mr. Speaker, you and the majority have gone too far. Even the sacred rules of golf have been violated.

For 5 long years you have had as the individual golf champion of Congress a member of your party, one MARTY RUSSO of Illinois. Now, when we, the Republicans, finally get a champion, me, who defeated your 5-year paragon of virtue, Mr. RUSSO, he will not abide by the rules and give me the winner's cup.

Even the rules of this sacred tournament have been violated. When, oh when, Mr. Speaker, will you make the members of your party abide by the sacred rules of this tournament?

I await with eager anticipation my trophy.

— Rep. Dan Burton (R-Ind.)
October 4, 1984

CANCELLED

Mr. DAVIS. Mr. Speaker, I take this time to announce today with great regret that a basketball game scheduled next week between the Democrats of the House and the Republicans of this House will not be played. Coach CONTE has forfeited.

After 12 years of handling the Democrats on the baseball field, Coach CONTE, unable to handle cotton uniforms, has decided that he will not be able to come to the court next week. I wish Coach CONTE good luck in trying to establish a north-south game or east-west game, but we on our side were planning to win this game just as we did the big game last November.

Mr. FLOWERS. Mr. Speaker, will the gentleman yield?

Mr. DAVIS. I yield to the gentleman from Alabama.

Mr. FLOWERS. Mr. Speaker, is the problem that the other side could find only five players and no substitutes? Or that they were fearful we might apply the 2 to 1 rule here, also?

Mr. DAVIS. They had five players, and we told them we were not going to play them 2 to 1, and that it would be even. I understand the regular substitutes, ERLENBORN and MICHEL, were ready as usual.

Mr. FLOWERS. I thank the gentleman.

Mr. HUNGATE. Mr. Speaker, will the gentleman yield?

Mr. DAVIS. I yield to the gentleman from Missouri.

Mr. HUNGATE. Mr. Speaker, I must have misunderstood, because I know the other side can always find a substitute.

Mr. DAVIS. I thank the gentleman. I know they can find a substitute. My only regret is that undoubtedly Coach CONTE also forfeited the right to come and rebut me here today, but they can always find outstanding pitchers such as the gentleman from Illinois (Mr. MICHEL) and the gentleman from Maine (Mr. COHEN). We will see those gentlemen in June on the diamond.

> — *Reps. Mendel J. Davis (D-S.C.), Walter Flowers (D-Ala.), and*
> *William L. Hungate (D-Mo.)*
> *April 10, 1975*

WRONG GAME, WRONG TIME

Mr. CONTE. Mr. Speaker, I note with pity that a Representative from King Cotton scolded me last Thursday for not fielding a Republican basketball team.

Do not let him pull the wool over your eyes. This is another case where the Democratic athletic supporters are stretching the truth.

First of all, who ever heard of starting a basketball season in late April? Only the Democratic leadership could come up with a schedule like that.

This stunt of wanting to play the wrong game at the wrong time is all too typical of the other side of the aisle.

I can see why the Democrats want to play basketball. Every time King Cotton blows the whistle, the majority jumps through a hoop. While the public sits on the sidelines waiting for action, the Democrats have been content to dribble around and sit on the ball.

They played that way through January, February, and March, but now we are in April, and the season has changed.

Now the majority should be taking the field every time King Caucus yells "play ball." If they are determined to copy their legislative procedures in a sporting event, they should be talking in terms of baseball.

They should no longer be showing the public how they can be dribbling around. They should be demonstrating their ability to be caught off base.

The gentleman's shot against me is not going to score any points or runs. His timing is too far off. His Democratic colleagues might say he has fouled out. On our side of the aisle, where we keep up with the times, we say he has struck out.

We are up with the times. We are looking forward to the annual congressional baseball game.

We will leave it to the Democrats to continue running back and forth, going nowhere, chasing a ball filled with something they already have plenty of—hot air.

—Rep. Silvio O. Conte (R-Mass.)
April 14, 1975

298-144

Mr. DAVIS. Mr. Speaker, I take this time just to announce to the Members of the House that the basketball game that was to be played last night between the Republicans and the Democrats has been officially forfeited. We had five Democrats show up at the Capital Centre; Coach CONTE sent no one. The Democrats showed up knowing the propensity of the Republicans for "dirty tricks." However, they were not bugged this time by Members of the opposition who would have been mere bugs on the water if they had opposed the dynamic Democratic basketball team.

The score now goes on the books as 289 to 144.

Mr. CONTE. Mr. Speaker, will the gentleman yield?

Mr. DAVIS. I yield to the gentleman from Massachusetts, and I am glad the gentleman has shown up to hear this announcement.

Mr. CONTE. Mr. Speaker, this is just more of that never-never world that the other side of the aisle is living in, a world of fantasy. Certainly we would have been there but, as I told the Members last week, the basket-ball season is over and, as usual, the Democrats are dribbling all around, playing the wrong game in the wrong season. We will meet you at the basketball park tonight, right now, tomorrow, or at any time.

Mr. DAVIS. The championship has not been decided as yet, and I would remind my friend that a team from Boston is still in the running.

Mr. CONTE. When it is time to plant cotton, as the distinguished gentle-man from South Carolina should know, it is time to start the baseball season, not basketball. But there are other reasons why the GOP stal-warts would not jump to the Democrats' whistle.

First, the gentleman has not been officially coronated as head basket-ball coach by King Caucus. Until this is done, his claim to be the legiti-mate coach for the majority is as thin as a fiber of cotton. I have noted how King Caucus treats even its powerful chairmen who seek authority to lead their committee teams. I pray their treatment of the gentleman who claims to lead their basketball team is a bit more charitable.

Instead of basketball, perhaps the gentleman should sponsor a con-gressional yo-yo tournament. That is one sport where the Democrats should win all the prizes. They have been going up and down so much recently every time King Caucus pulls the string that by now they resem-ble a yo-yo in action.

— Reps. Silvio O. Conte (R-Mass.) and Mendel J. Davis (D-S.C.)
April 17, 1975

BIRD LIVES

Mr. CONTE. Mr. Speaker, in the Middle Ages, they were called Keltics—Celtics—the great Irish warriors. Living up to their namesakes last night in Boston Garden, the Boston Celtics captured their 15th world championship banner by smashing the L.A. Lakers, 111-102. In this thrill-ing series, the Celtics showed the Nation that perseverance, when com-bined with a multitude of talent and a great coach, is what leads to the glory.

Standing head and shoulders over even his tallest adversaries, howev-er, is perhaps the greatest player that ever lived, Larry Bird. With the sighting of a hawk, the arm span of an eagle, and the humility of an ostrich, Larry Bird has shown the doubters what being a good, clean, professional sportsman is all about.

Cedric Maxwell's performance last night was nothing less than stellar, as well, scoring 24 points against a tough Lakers defense.

I salute the world champion Celtics on their great series victory last night, and join with the people of the State of Massachusetts and the city of Boston in singing their praises.

Mr. LUNGREN. Mr. Speaker, will the gentleman from Massachusetts yield?

Mr. CONTE. Yes, I yield to the gentleman from California.

Mr. LUNGREN. I just wonder—the gentleman is on the Appropriations Committee and I wonder if he has given any thought to a Federal grant to provide air conditioning at Boston Garden, so that those poor players from the west coast who are used to heat but not humidity might be able to play on an equal playing field next time around?

Mr. CONTE. My warriors do not need air conditioning. In fact, it's unfortunate that we ever got it here in the Capitol. We would be out of here by now.

— Reps. Silvio O. Conte (R-Mass.) and Dan Lungren (R-Calif.)
June 13, 1984

SENATE RESOLUTION 162

Mr. D'AMATO submitted the following resolution; which was referred to the Committee on Labor and Human Resources:

S. RES. 162

Whereas, the major league baseball strike has covered the hearts and minds of Americans like an infield tarpaulin in a summer shower, life in America has been adversely affected in several ways:

Trading baseball cards has become as meaningful as swapping gas coupons,

Youngsters now yearn to be federal mediators rather than the next Joe Dimaggio,

Billy Martin has not dusted the trousers of an umpire for several days,
The economy has been slowed by a decline in the sales of hot dogs, peanuts, beer, and soda pop,
The Chicago Cubs have not lost a game in nearly three weeks,
Americans are being bombarded with television reruns and old movies,
Divorce rates are soaring as husbands and wives are being forced to pay attention to each other,
Americans even miss Howard Cosell,
The God-given right of New Yorkers to have a team, if not two, in the World Series is threatened,

Therefore, be it resolved that it is the sense of the Senate that a summer day in America is not complete without the cry of "Play ball." The major league owners and players should let boys be boys, reach an equitable agreement, as soon as possible and return the "Boys of Summer" to America.

—Alfonse M. D'Amato (R-N.Y.)
June 25, 1981

THERE OUGHTA BE A LAW?

On pay toilets
and other pressing matters

THERE
OUGHTA
BE A
LAW?

FREE TO GO

Mr. JOHN L. BURTON. Mr. Chairman, I offer an amendment.
The Clerk read as follows:

Amendment offered by Mr. JOHN L. BURTON: Page 21, Title II, after Section 203, immediately after line 18, insert the following new Section:

SEC. 204(a). No funds appropriated by this Act shall be made available by means of any grant, contract, loan, or other contribution or expenditure for the construction, maintenance, or operation of, or for other use with respect to, any facility or building containing pay toilets.
(b) As used in this section, the term pay toilet means a water closet in any restroom or lavatory facility which imposes a fee, by coin deposit or otherwise, as a condition of access to or use of said water closet.

Mr. BAUMAN. Mr. Chairman, I reserve a point of order on the amendment.
The CHAIRMAN. The gentleman from Maryland (Mr. BAUMAN) reserves a point of order on the amendment.
The gentleman from California (Mr. JOHN L. BURTON) is recognized for 5 minutes in support of his amendment.
Mr. JOHN L. BURTON. Mr. Chairman, Members, I will be very brief. We have talked about a lot of issues today and yesterday. I think this is really one of the gut issues facing this Congress.
We have talked about taxation. We have talked about progressive and regressive taxation. Certainly, I think forcing taxpayers to pay their own money out of their own pockets in a building that is paid for by their own

taxes for the purposes of answering nature's call is a very restrictive form of taxation.

We have had this law on the books of the great State of California and it has worked very well. We know that the great mayor of the great city of Chicago, Mayor Daley, has instituted such a policy. I feel that it is a proper policy to be instituted by the Congress in federally financed buildings....

Mr. Chairman, I yield back the balance of my time.

The CHAIRMAN. Does the gentleman from Maryland insist on his point of order?

Mr. BAUMAN. I would not dare, Mr. Chairman....

Mr. JACOBS. Mr. Chairman, I move to strike the last word.

I regret, Mr. Chairman, being placed in the position of having the last word on this amendment, especially since I have just moved to strike the last word on this amendment.

I promised my colleague from California, who shall remain nameless to protect the record, that I will not say anything about the fact that when I rose, his face was flushed, but his broad shoulders saved him.

I would like to rise in defense of Jack Benny, who is deceased. For years there has been a story going around that I have reason to believe just is not true, and that is that Jack Benny invented limbo dancing while entering a pay toilet in Lima, Ohio.

Mr. Chairman, I yield back the remainder of my time.

—Reps. John L. Burton (D-Calif.), Robert E. Bauman (R-Md.), and
Andrew Jacobs, Jr. (D-Ind.)
November 13, 1975

TOUCHY-FEELY

Mr. WYLIE. Mr. Chairman, I offer an amendment.
The Clerk read as follows:

Amendment offered by Mr. WYLIE: Page 20, line 10, strike out $33,864,000 "and insert in lieu thereof $33,761,000."

Mr. WYLIE. Mr. Chairman, this is a copy of Playboy reproduced in braille by the Library of Congress with taxpayers' money. This is an example of your taxpayers' money at work.

[Laughter, Members moved to the desk to pick up copies.]

Mr. WYLIE. It will not help you, gentlemen, it will not help you unless you can read braille. Gentlemen, this is a serious amendment, and I do not regard it as a joke. The only joke is that taxpayers' moneys are involved in reproducing Playboy in braille.

> — *Rep. Chalmers P. Wylie (R-Ohio)*
> *July 18, 1985*

DRESSED TO KILL

Mr. BIAGGI. Mr. Speaker, today I am introducing legislation which is aimed at keeping bulletproof vests off of criminals in the United States. Under my bill, a bulletproof vest would be redefined as a firearm....

> — *Rep. Mario Biaggi (D-N.Y.)*
> *November 16, 1981*

NOT-SO-SECRET SERVICE

H.R. 7349
The Former Presidential Enough Is Enough and
Taxpayers Relief Act of 1980.

IN THE HOUSE OF REPRESENTATIVES
May 14, 1980

Mr. JACOBS introduced the following bill; which was referred to the Committee on Government Operations

A BILL
The Former Presidential Enough Is Enough and
Taxpayers Relief Act of 1980.

Be it enacted by the Senate and House of Representatives of the United States of America in Congress assembled, That the total annual Government expenditures for the care and feeding of a former President shall not exceed ten times the poverty level income for one urban family of four.

— Rep. Andrew Jacobs, Jr. (D-Ind.)
May 14, 1980

FLYING HIGH

Mr. ABERNETHY. Mr. Speaker, by direction of the Committee on the District of Columbia I call up the bill (H.R. 16476) to make it lawful to set up or fly any kite in the District of Columbia, and ask unanimous consent that the bill be considered in the House as in Committee of the Whole....

Mr. JACOBS. Mr. Speaker, I rise in support of this legislation, and point out to the House that here in the capital of the free world there is no freedom to do the most 100 percent American thing that an American citizen can do—go fly a kite.

I do not intend to make a "long-winded" speech about this, Mr. Speaker, but a grave situation does exist in the District of Columbia, and the District of Columbia local government, the Department of the Interior, and the Smithsonian Institution have all requested this legislation.

Mr. Speaker, there is more danger in the existing law than one might imagine. For example, if one citizen were to tell another to go out and fly a kite, he would be advocating the commission of a crime in the District of Columbia. I doubt that this ever happens in the District of Columbia, but just in case any citizen ever got high as a kite he would be in double jeopardy.

I do not want to shock anybody, but Benjamin Franklin would be out of luck in his Nation's Capital today.

I realize that there are other provisions in the same law that have raised some question this very morning—the same law that we are dealing with makes a crime of causing a dog to bite or setting dogs on persons or animals—the more I think about it I think it is a good provision.

Fastening horses to trees is also outlawed by this statute.

Also, it is a crime to drive a vehicle in excess of 12 miles per hour outside of Georgetown or in excess of 8 miles per hour inside of Georgetown.

So we have a long way to go, really. As President Kennedy said, a journey of a thousand miles begins with a single step, and I give the House my assurance, as the author of this bill, that I as an individual will look into these other matters if you will just help get this one off the ground.

Mr. HALL. Mr. Speaker, will the gentleman yield?

Mr. JACOBS. I yield to the gentleman from Missouri.

Mr. HALL. Mr. Speaker, I certainly want to commend the gentleman for his "erudite" presentation. Furthermore I think that the gentleman is very generous in contriving this bill, and I am glad that he pointed out Benjamin Franklin's propensities and the difficulties that he would encounter if he was in the District of Columbia today. They are modest as to natural lightening.

But, I wonder if the gentleman does not really think that this legislation is inspired, whether it is in his extrasensory perception or his subconscious mind or not, by instructions perhaps of the current President to his Secretary of the Interior? What I am really trying to say is: Did he tell Secretary of the Interior Hickel to "go fly a kite," and that that is the real reason for this legislation?

Mr. JACOBS. I plead the constitutional right not to interfere with another branch of Government, and I ask the gentleman to excuse me from answering the question, although according to the press that may well be true.

Mr. HALL. Mr. Speaker, I would be the last to ask that this distinguished "jurist" now in the well of the House forgo the principle of the sovereignty of powers. If I have erred in this direction, I want to withdraw and retract that. But I have heard it rumored in certain circles—

Mr. JACOBS. Is the gentleman saying that rumors are flying?

Mr. HALL. Yes, like father flown kites in Missouri springtime on Mother's Day. I have heard it rumored in certain circles that he is going to devote all of his personal memoranda paper to Chairman of the City Council, Washington, to be used in kite manufacturing process, and we the Congress must have surveillance and review over the process that might involve a "conflict of interest." I certainly do not believe we should take all of this paper from the Department of the Interior and turn it into kites just because of the gentleman's bill. It would be like propelling a steam engine with the hot air emanating from these Chambers.

Mr. JACOBS. I know of the gentleman's admiration for some of the local newspapers and I might suggest a good use for them in this way.

Mr. HALL. I think that would clash with "red sails in the sunset." I thank the gentleman.

Mr. HUNGATE. Mr. Speaker, will the gentleman yield?

Mr. JACOBS. I yield to the Will Rogers of Missouri.

Mr. HUNGATE. I will have to tell a story if you are going to do that.

But, Mr. Speaker, I would like to commend the gentleman on bringing this bill to the floor because I am sure—

Mr. JACOBS. The gentleman surely means "bringing up" this bill.

Mr. HUNGATE. Yes, I thank my colleague.

I think that is eloquent testimony to the wisdom of our retaining home rule right here in this Chamber so we can pass on kite flying.

—Reps. Thomas G. Abernethy (D-Miss.), Andrew Jacobs, Jr. (D-Ind.), Durward
G. Hall (R-Mo.), and William L. Hungate (D-Mo.)
May 11, 1970

WINNIE LEFT HER BEHIND

The Senate proceeded to consider the bill (S. 1602) authorizing and directing the Secretary of the Interior to issue to Winnie Left Her Behind a patent in fee to certain land, which was read as follows:

Be it enacted, etc., That the Secretary of the Interior is authorized and directed to issue to Winnie Left Her Behind, a Sioux Indian of the Rosebud Indian Reservation, S. Dak., a patent in fee to the northeast quarter of section 25, township 42, range 31 east, of the Black Hills meridian.

Mr. WHERRY. Mr. President, may we have an explanation of the bill?

Mr. BUSHFIELD. Do I understand the Senator from Nebraska to request an explanation of the bill?

The ACTING PRESIDENT pro tempore. The Chair so understands.

Mr. BUSHFIELD. Mr. President, as I look over various names on the calendar, I see names such as Pokluda and Buby and Paluck, and even when I look around the Senate, right back of me I see individuals with names just as peculiar as the name "Winnie Left Her Behind." I assure the Senate that out in the open spaces of South Dakota the Sioux Indians pick appropriate names which mean something. Whether Winnie was left behind by someone who went away, and left her in custody of another, or whether the name refers to someone else, whom Winnie left behind her, I do not know. I think we should leave the interpretation of the name to the Senator himself. However, Winnie Left Her Behind is her name.

—Sens. Kenneth S. Wherry (R-Nebr.) and Harlan J. Bushfield (R-S.D.)
May 25, 1944

FOR BETTER OR FOR WORSE

Mr. HUMPHREY. Do I correctly understand that under the terms of the bill the Attorney General is to have something to say about whether or not a marriage relationship has been fulfilled and is satisfactory? Will the Senator give me that information again? That certainly smacks of something new in legislation.

Mr. MOODY. It certainly smacks of something. The bill provides that if a bride and bridegroom come into this country under a marriage relationship, and fail to fulfill the marital agreement to the satisfaction of the Attorney General—

Mr. HUMPHREY. Just a moment. Let us stop there.

Mr. MOODY. I do not know why the Attorney General should be interested in that, but perhaps he is.

Mr. HUMPHREY. I know that many people have had unkind words to say about many Attorneys General, but I do not believe Congress ought to put the burden upon the Attorney General to decide whether a marriage relationship is satisfactory or has been properly consummated.

Mr. MOODY. That is my point.

Mr. HUMPHREY. What is the express language again?

Mr. MOODY. "Fail to fulfill marital agreements to the satisfaction of the Attorney General."

Mr. HUMPHREY. I think we should ascertain from the sponsors of the bill just what that means. It sounds very interesting.

Mr. MOODY. It would be interesting to know.

Mr. HUMPHREY. I should like to know what it means.

Mr. MOODY. I do not think the proponents of the bill can tell us; but, if the Senator desires to ask them, he may do so.

Mr. HUMPHREY. The Attorney General is going to be a busy man, under this bill.

Mr. MOODY. He certainly is.

Mr. HUMPHREY. Not only that, he is going to be in on some secrets he ought not to be in on.

Mr. MOODY. The Senator is correct.

Mr. PASTORE. Mr. President, will the Senator yield?

Mr. MOODY. I am delighted to yield.

Mr. PASTORE. As a matter of fact, the McCarran bill may become the best seller of the year.

Mr. HUMPHREY. It will certainly become a sort of congressional Kinsey report.

> *—Sen. Hubert H. Humphrey (D-Minn.), Blair Moody (D-Mich.), and*
> *John O. Pastore (D-R.I.)*
> *May 15, 1952*

**SAY
AMEN,
SOMEBODY**

Let us pray

SAY
AMEN,
SOMEBODY

A GREAT FALL

The Chaplain, the Reverend Richard C. Halverson, D.D., offered the following prayer:

Let us pray.
Humpty Dumpty sat on a wall. Humpty Dumpty had a great fall. All the king's horses and all the king's men couldn't put Humpty Dumpty together again.

Dear God, in mercy and grace, prevent the Senate from being like Humpty Dumpty. Keep it from being so fractured and fragmented that no one will be able to put it together again....

— The Rev. Richard C. Halverson
April 5, 1983

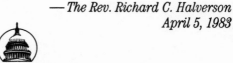

FIDDLING AROUND

The Chaplain, the Reverend Richard C. Halverson, D.D., offered the following prayer:

Let us pray.
Dear God, help the Senate to comprehend its potential: One hundred intelligent, reasonable, thoughtful, strong gentle people, each rich in credentials. Individually each is a rational person but somehow in the chem-

istry of the body very irrational things happen, its benign chemicals, which when mixed, cause an explosion; or explosive chemicals, when mixed, neutralize each other.

One hundred well-qualified people, a symphony orchestra capable of producing a symphony but sounding much of the time like they are tuning up for a concert.

Help them, Lord, to find their harmony, so together they can make beautiful music to bless the Nation and the world. In the name of One whose mission was to unite all peoples. Amen.

RECOGNITION OF THE MAJORITY LEADER

The PRESIDENT pro tempore. The majority leader is recognized.
Mr. BAKER. I thank the Chair.

THE MAJORITY LEADER COMMENTS ON THE CHAPLAIN'S PRAYER

Mr. BAKER. Mr. President, I must say to our distinguished and illustrious Chaplain that as far as this Member of the orchestra is concerned, there are many days, including this one, when I would settle not only for beautiful music but for any music at all. I would also observe for the benefit of the Chaplain, if we run completely out of music we can always call on the minority leader and his expert fiddling in the field of bluegrass music.

Mr. President, that is probably the last kind word I will have to say all day long.

— *The Rev. Richard C. Halverson and Sen. Howard H. Baker, Jr. (R-Tenn.)*
July 15, 1983

TALKIN' TRASH

The Chaplain, the Reverend Richard C. Halverson, D.D., offered the following prayer:

Let us pray.
God of Abraham, Isaac, and Israel, God of our Lord Jesus Christ, the

apostles and the church, the Senate meets this morning midst compounding frustration: Family pleasure postponed, important trips canceled, many plans aborted. No one is happy about this, least of all the leadership. But, dear Lord, Thou dost often turn disappointment into significant achievement. Thy word declares, "God works in everything for good to those who love Him and are called according to His purpose." (Romans 8:28.)

If man can recycle junk and transform it to useful purpose, certainly Thou, O God, can transform disappointment and frustration into very special blessing. Surprise the Senate today Lord, with Thy peace and grace and love. Make this a day which all who are disappointed will remember with profound gratitude as one of significant achievement. We pray this in the name of Him who was a model of tranquility midst the worst possible circumstances. Amen.

RECOGNITION OF THE MAJORITY LEADER

The PRESIDENT pro tempore. The majority leader is recognized.
Mr. BAKER. I thank the Chair.

CHAPLAIN COMMENDED ON OPENING PRAYER

Mr. BAKER. Mr. President, I commend the Chaplain on his prayer. I have to confess that as is often the case, as I always do, I listen carefully to the Chaplain's prayer. I try to assimilate every word. I try not to read secondary meaning into his words and his supplications to the Lord, but I could not resist wondering whose junk he was talking about.

—*The Rev. Richard C. Halverson and Sen. Howard H. Baker, Jr. (R-Tenn.)*
July 16, 1983

TECHNICALITIES

The Chaplain, the Reverend Richard C. Halverson, D.D., offered the following prayer:

Let us pray.
Unless the Lord watches over the city, the watchman stays awake in vain.—Psalm 127:1 (RSV).
Sovereign Lord, no individual or group of individuals take more seriously national security than the Senate....

RECOGNITION OF THE MAJORITY LEADER

The PRESIDENT pro tempore. The majority leader is recognized.
Mr. BAKER. Mr. President, I thank the Chair.

EXCEPT THE LORD KEEP THE CITY

Mr. BAKER. Mr. President, the minority leader makes me feel inadequate in many ways, most often in terms of our comparative knowledge of the rules and precedents of the Senate. But I have to confess that I was simply overwhelmed this morning when my friend the minority leader turned to me and said our distinguished Chaplain did not use the King James version this morning. I not only feel inadequate. I feel guilty.
Mr. BYRD. Will the majority leader yield?
Mr. BAKER. Yes, I yield.
Mr. BYRD. In the King James version, the passage is this: "Except the Lord keep the city, the watchman waketh but in vain."
Mr. BAKER. I have an Apple computer at home, Mr. President, but it is not that good.
Mr. BYRD. I did not mean to be critical of the Chaplain. I just wanted to comment.

—The Rev. Richard C. Halverson and Sens. Howard H. Baker, Jr. (R-Tenn.) and
Robert C. Byrd (D-W. Va.)
July 20, 1983

DIVINE INTERVENTION

The Chaplain, the Reverend Richard C. Halverson, D.D., offered the following prayer:

Let us pray.
God of our nations, who has ordained governments as Thy ministers

for good, we thank Thee for our political system, born out of profound struggle. We thank Thee that the people are sovereign and that public servants must defend their records at regular intervals. We pray for those Members of the Senate whose records will be tested in November. Help them to distinguish between what must be done here and now and what can better wait for the next Congress. Give them grace to deal with the tension between their perception of what the people want and the real issues which will be determinative.

Loving Father, help the people to understand and appreciate the ambivalence and struggle which our system imposes upon incumbents. Help the people to make their judgments upon the basis of integrity rather than single issues. Guide the Senators who are candidates—give special wisdom to their organizations and help them raise the funds necessary for their campaigns. In His name in whom resides all authority. Amen.

RECOGNITION OF THE MAJORITY LEADER

The PRESIDENT pro tempore. The majority leader is recognized.

THE CHAPLAIN'S PRAYER

Mr. BAKER. Mr. President, I call the Chaplain's attention to the fact that what he has done perhaps must be reported on the Federal Election Commission form for every Member of the Senate who is seeking reelection, as a contribution in kind. But if there is a topical prayer and one relevant to the concerns of many Members, I do not believe I have ever heard the Lord asked to make sure that we raise enough money to conduct our campaigns. However, I admire the technique.

— *The Rev. Richard C. Halverson and Sen. Howard H. Baker, Jr. (R-Tenn.)*
May 22, 1984

CONFESSION

The Chaplain, the Reverend Richard C. Halverson, D.D., offered the following prayer:

Let us pray.

God of order, truth and justice, despite my political naivete, I sense that the leadership of the Senate identifies with the feelings of Cicero, the great Roman statesman of the first century B.C., when he said, "The first of June and nothing done by the Senate."

Thou knowest all things, omniscient God. The future is as plain to Thee as the past. No detail escapes Thy notice. Days pass swiftly and they are few before recess. Give to the leadership Thy wisdom in scheduling priorities involving many agendas, all of which are important to those whose they are.

Lord of life, Thy word declares, "A man's mind plans his way, but the Lord directs his steps." (Prov. 16: 9 RSV). Guide the Senate in its business so that in these next 3 weeks everything that ought to be done will be. To the glory of Thy name. Amen.

RECOGNITION OF THE MAJORITY LEADER

The PRESIDENT pro tempore. The majority leader is recognized.

THE CHAPLAIN'S PRAYER

Mr. BAKER. Mr. President, I sometimes make facetious and flip remarks about our good Chaplain's prayers. I cannot help this morning succumbing to that temptation again. I suppose this is a good time for confession, so to speak. I confess I have never before thought of any similarity between me and Cicero. But if Cicero indeed said that, Cicero was plenty right and knew what he was talking about.

— *The Rev. Richard C. Halverson and Sen. Howard H. Baker, Jr. (R-Tenn.)*
June 7, 1984

THE FIXER

Mr. HUGH SCOTT. Mr. President, in his prayer this morning, the Chaplain included a solicitation to the Almighty "for those who service our homes."

Maybe that is the only way to do it. I have been waiting for a long time for someone to fix the icemaker and a longer time for someone to paint the house.

I have tried everything short of prayer. I am, therefore, very thankful to the Chaplain for his suggestion.

— Sen. Hugh Scott (R-Pa.)
June 24, 1974

THE FINAL SESSION

O Supreme Legislator ... Make seniority in Your love ever germane to their conduct. Make them consistently vote yea in the cloakroom of conscience that at the expiration of life's term they may feel no need to revise and extend....

When the Congress of life is adjourned and they answer the final quorum call, may the eternal committee report out a clean bill on their lives.

—Name and date unknown

WHO'S ON FIRST?

Disorder in the House . . . and Senate

WHO'S
ON
FIRST?

WHAT THE HECK

Mr. ECKHARDT. Mr. Chairman, as I understand what the gentleman is doing, the amendment is saying that 4 years after any particular mileage standard required for an entire fleet of cars, then there may not be any car distributed which exceeds that figure to which the limitation was placed 4 years earlier on the entire fleet, and if it is attempted to sell a car which does not meet that standard, the company may be enjoined from selling it?

Mr. JACOBS. By action of the Justice Department; the gentleman is right.

Mr. ECKHARDT. And in addition to that, this only applies to passenger vehicles; is that correct?

Mr. JACOBS. Well, I do not know just what that means—but yes, what the heck.

— *Reps. Bob Eckhardt (D-Texas) and Andrew Jacobs, Jr. (D-Ind.)*
June 12, 1975

TO SLEEP, PERCHANCE TO VOTE

Mr. PASTORE. This is the most interesting part of the day. Let us proceed.

Mr. HUGH SCOTT. I am glad we are keeping the Senator from Rhode Island awake.

Mr. PASTORE. No; you are not keeping me awake. I get up at 5:30 in the morning, and I go to bed at 10 at night, and after 5:30 in the morning I am absolutely awake. I will be delighted if the Senator from Pennsylvania wishes to take a run around the block with me.

Mr. HUGH SCOTT. If the Senator from Rhode Island wishes to divert me, I will give him whatever time he needs, after which I will return to my question.

Mr. PASTORE. You may be asleep, but I am not.

Mr. HUGH SCOTT. I assure the Senator that I was not asleep when I voted on this ballot.

Mr. PASTORE. I know, but I think you are asleep now. Go ahead.

Mr. HUGH SCOTT. Will the Senator allow me to proceed on the time that has been ruled to me?

Mr. PASTORE. That is right, provided you are awake.

Mr. HUGH SCOTT. If the Senator will restrain himself for a moment.

Mr. PASTORE. I do not have to restrain myself, but I think it is very discourteous on the part of the Senator from Pennsylvania—

Mr. HUGH SCOTT. Mr. President, who has the floor?

> —*Sens. John O. Pastore (D-R.I.) and Hugh Scott (R-Pa.)*
> *June 23, 1975*

A LARGE BODY OF SILENCE

Mr. HELMS. Mr. President, I reserve the remainder of my time.

The PRESIDING OFFICER. Who yields time? If neither side yields time, time runs equally.

Mr. PRYOR. Mr. President, will the Chair please inform at least this Senator as to what is going on in the Senate at this moment?

The PRESIDING OFFICER. The Chair states that we are in a unanimous consent time agreement on the Helms amendment, and unless either Senator HELMS or Senator HATCH yields time, the time is running equally.

Mr. PRYOR. There seems to be a large body of silence at this moment, Mr. President, and I was very curious. It is rare that we have this degree of silence in the Senate Chamber.

Mr. HELMS. Enjoy it while you can.

Mr. PRYOR. I just rise on a point of curiosity, I say to my friend from North Carolina.

Mr. HELMS. Mr. President, I am going to yield back the remainder of my time, if there is no objection to the amendment. This is a delightful set of circumstances.

—Sens. Jesse Helms (R-N.C.) and David Pryor (D-Ark.)
October 2, 1986

LATIN LOVER

Mr. HUGH SCOTT. Mr. President, I will stay within the time, although it will be difficult....

NORRIS COTTON is of a notably gentle, tolerant, and patient disposition. He does not need to apologize to us.

Our old friend and colleague Cicero said about men like NORRIS COTTON:

Vir et fortissimus in publica et firmissimus in resuscepta.

I ask unanimous consent to include the translation as soon as I can find it. [Laughter.]

—Sen. Hugh Scott (R-Pa.)
September 18, 1974

A BRIEF SCUFFLE

[About a quarter past eleven o'clock, after prayers, whilst the SPEAKER was in his Chair, and many members in their places, but before the House had been called to order, and before the Journal had been read, Mr. GRISWOLD entered the House, and observing Mr. LYON in his place (who was writing) he went up to him with a pretty strong walking stick in his hand, with which he immediately began to beat him with great violence. Mr. G.'s approach was observed by Mr. LYON, but before he could get from behind his desk he had received some severe blows. As soon as he got on the floor of the House he endeavored to lay hold of Mr. G. (having no stick or weapon in his hand) but he was prevented from doing so by Mr. G.'s falling back, and the continual blows with which he was assailed. At length getting behind the Speaker's chair, Mr. L. snatched up the tongs from the fire; the combatants then closed and came down together upon the floor, Mr. G. being uppermost. The members in the House, who till now seemed to look on with amazement at the scene, without an attempt to put an end to it, got round the parties, and separated them, but not before Mr. L. had aimed a blow at Mr. G.'s head with the tongs, but which he parried off. The SPEAKER was now called upon to desire the members to take their seats, and form the House. Whilst this was doing, the two enraged members met again without the bar, and but for the doorkeeper and some gentlemen present, would have renewed the combat. Order having been obtained (at least as much as it was possible to obtain from the agitated state of the House) the Clerk proceeded to read the Journal, and the business of the day was entered upon....]

> *—Reps. Roger Griswold (F-Ct.) and Matthew Lyon (F-Vt.)*
> *Annals of Congress, February 15, 1798*

LET ME MAKE ONE MORE RUN AT THIS MATTER

Mr. HELMS. I do not want to ask the leader to confide in me anything I am not supposed to know. But did the Speaker indicate the House is not going to act on the resolution of disapproval at all?

Mr. BYRD. I will not divulge a private conversation that I may have had with the Senator from North Carolina, and I will not divulge a private conversation with the Speaker of the House of Representatives.

Mr. HELMS. OK. Well, I think I prefaced it by saying I did not want the distinguished Democratic leader to discuss anything that was of a private nature.

Mr. BYRD. The able Senator did say that.

Mr. HELMS. Of course this is sort of a public nature, too.

Mr. BYRD. It is. Yes. It is of a public nature. The Senator is within his right to ask me the question.

Mr. HELMS. The Senator is within his right not to answer me.

Mr. BYRD. It is not a matter of my right. I am asserting here that if I have a private conversation with Mr. DOLE, or any other Member of Congress, I would rather not divulge that.

Mr. HELMS. I am trying to find out whether the House is going to do anything or not....

Let me make one more run at this matter to my friend from West Virginia who was born in North Carolina.

Mr. BYRD. The motto of which State it is "To be rather than to seem."

Mr. HELMS. Yes. Esse Quam Videri. The Senator is right.

Suppose there should be an opportunity to wager on the possibility of the House acting on the resolution of disapproval before the deadline early next week. How would the Senator advise me to bet?

[Laughter.]

I do not ask him to disclose anything of a confidential nature with the Speaker.

Mr. BYRD. I understand. Well, I can recall a quotation from Shakespeare on that point. I can recall at the moment that he did say, "Neither a borrower nor a lender be; For loan oft loses both itself and friend, and borrowing dulls the edge of husbandry."

He did not say anything that I recall about wagering. I do not wager. I learned when I was growing up that I did not have money to throw away. Nickels came pretty hard. I am sure the Senator from North Carolina found it the same way.

If I was able to get a bottle of pop a year—they called it a bottle of pop, Coca-Cola or something else—I was pretty lucky. An ice cream cone cost 5 cents. I could go to the store for the lady next door and she would give me a nickel, and I recall on one occasion buying a cone of ice cream, talking to someone, and the cone tipped, the ice cream dropped on the ground, and I made up my mind then and there that I would eat all of the ice cream I could eat if I lived to be a man and had a few nickels to spare.

So I do not wager. Why do I not wager? Because I might lose my nickels.

So my suggestion to the distinguished Senator would be that he not wager on this matter. He may not win any money, but he certainly will save his own.

Mr. HELMS. My father made the same suggestion, I might say. He put a little more oomph behind it. He flatly said "Do not bet." I do not. So I join the Senator in not being a wagering man.

—Sens. Jesse Helms (R-N.C.) and Robert C. Byrd (D-W. Va.)
January 29, 1987

ORDER, PLEASE

Mr. NELSON. Mr. President, may we have order?

The PRESIDING OFFICER. Will those Senators having discussions please retire to the cloakroom so the clerk can call the roll and the Senators can reply?

Mr. NELSON. I think the Chair should speak more loudly. Some of the Senators have their hearing aids turned off.

The PRESIDING OFFICER. The Senator from Wisconsin was correct.

The Senate will be in order.

Mr. PASTORE. Mr. President, I cannot understand it. When the Chair orders people to take their seats, they just keep strolling around. Can they just take their seats and let us have our business done with?

The PRESIDING OFFICER. I agree with the distinguished Senator.

The Senators will please take their seats or go out and read the Washington Post, or whatever they want to read.

—Sens. Gaylord Nelson (D-Wis.), Thomas J. McIntyre (D-N.H.)
(Presiding Officer), and John O. Pastore (D-R.I.)
December 14, 1974

PARLIAMENTARY INQUIRY

Mr. LOTT. Mr. Speaker, who is in charge? What are we doing here?

The SPEAKER pro tempore. The House is waiting on what business the Senate may send us, among other things. We are not sure what the Senate may send us.

Mr. LOTT. Well, do we know what they are going to send us? I mean, I understand that they are punting back the reconciliation package, insisting on the original language with the idea that they are not going to take up the unanimous consent cigarette tax and other things we just agreed to, and I do not see that as much of a bluff. So why are we here?

The SPEAKER pro tempore. The Chair is not privy to what the Senate is doing at this time.

— Rep. Trent Lott (R-Miss.)
December 19, 1985

WHO HAS THE FLOOR?

The PRESIDING OFFICER. A quorum is present.

Mr. DOUGLAS and Mr. KEFAUVER addressed the Chair.

The PRESIDING OFFICER. The Senator from Illinois is recognized.

Mr. DOUGLAS. I will yield to the Senator from Tennessee.

Mr. MORSE. Is the Senator yielding?

Mr. MANSFIELD. Mr. President, a parliamentary inquiry.

The PRESIDING OFFICER. The Senator will state it.

Mr. MANSFIELD. Can the Senator from Illinois yield to the Senator from Tennessee?

Mr. MORSE. That is the point I raise.

The PRESIDING OFFICER. The Senator can yield for a question but not for a statement, if some Senator makes a point of order.

Mr. MORSE. Mr. President, a parliamentary inquiry.

The PRESIDING OFFICER. The Senator will state it.

Mr. MORSE. Who has the floor?

The PRESIDING OFFICER. The Senator from Illinois.

Mr. KERR. Mr. President, a parliamentary inquiry.

Mr. DOUGLAS. Mr. President, a parliamentary inquiry. Who has the floor?

The PRESIDING OFFICER. The Senator from Illinois has the floor.

Mr. DOUGLAS. I should like to continue, if I may.

Mr. LONG of Louisiana. Mr. President, will the Senator yield?

Mr. DOUGLAS. If I yield I lose the floor, and I shall have to recover it again.

Mr. LONG of Louisiana. The Senator can yield on his own time.

Mr. DOUGLAS. I yield on my time.

Mr. LONG of Louisiana. Can the Senator correct me about the wording of the ancient English poem—

Mr. KUCHEL. Mr. President, I call for the regular order.

Mr. LONG of Louisiana. Cannot the Senator yield for a question on his own time?

The PRESIDING OFFICER. The Senator can yield for a question on his own time.

Mr. DOUGLAS. I yield for a question on my own time.

Mr. LONG of Louisiana. Can the Senator correct me on the wording of that ancient poem which goes something like this:

The law locks up—
Mr. DOUGLAS—
Both man and woman—
Mr. LONG of Louisiana—
Who steals the goose—
Mr. DOUGLAS—
From off the common—
Mr. LONG of Louisiana—
But then turns loose—
Mr. DOUGLAS—
But lets the greater felon loose,
Who steals the common from the goose.

Mr. LONG of Louisiana. Right.

Mr. DOUGLAS. That is an appropriate question at such a time as this.

Mr. KUCHEL. Mr. President, that is a joint question and a joint answer.

Mr. DOUGLAS. Mr. President, I ask if I am still recognized.

—*Sens. Paul H. Douglas (D-Ill.), Wayne L. Morse (D-Oreg.), Mike Mansfield (D-Mont.), Robert S. Kerr (D-Okla.), Russell B. Long (D-La.), and Thomas H. Kuchel (R-Calif.)*
August 15, 1962

MR. STOCKMAN

Mr. HOLLINGS. With respect to the strategy of the distinguished Senator from New York about David Stockman, I only remind the distinguished Senator from New York that Stockman was his student, not mine. I never did believe him.

Mr. MOYNIHAN. Will the Senator yield for a comment on a point of personal privilege?

Mr. HOLLINGS. Yes.

Mr. MOYNIHAN. Mr. Stockman was my babysitter, not my student.

Mr. HOLLINGS. The Senator from New York told us he was his student. If he was his babysitter, I would not trust him with the baby.

Mr. MOYNIHAN. On a personal point of privilege, I did not say anything of the kind one way or the other.

Mr. HOLLINGS. There is no need to make a personal privilege about it. The Senator is the one who told me about his relationship with Mr. Stockman. I am not making it up.

Mr. MOYNIHAN. On a point of personal privilege, does the Senator suggest that I ever said Mr. Stockman was a student? A student is someone who comes to classes.

Mr. HOLLINGS. I misunderstood. I thought the Senator said he was a student under the Senator. He was a babysitter. The Senator told me that.

Mr. MOYNIHAN. Yes. He lived with us. I was very happy to have him. In return for living quarters, his principal responsibilities were to do babysitting occasionally.

Mr. HOLLINGS. But in any event, I would not trust him with the baby. [Laughter.]

—*Sens. Ernest F. Hollings (D-S.C.) and Daniel Patrick Moynihan (D-N.Y.)*
July 23, 1986

THE STATUS QUO

Mr. HUGH SCOTT. Mr. President, first I congratulate the Presiding Officer and myself on being present.

Second, I wonder who else is.

Third, I am afraid to count. [Laughter.]

Fourth, there may be a quorum.

Fifth, as the late General Eisenhower used to say, the obvious we confuse immediately. The crystal clear takes a little longer. [Laughter.]

— Sen. Hugh Scott (R-Pa.)
October 17, 1974

FLOOD CONTROL

Mr. ROUSSELOT. Mr. Chairman, will the gentleman yield?

Mr. FLOOD. I yield to the gentleman from California.

Mr. ROUSSELOT. Mr. Chairman, would the gentleman read that for us again where it says the school district is prohibited from keeping records?

Mr. FLOOD. Can you not read it?

Mr. ROUSSELOT. Read it.

Mr. FLOOD. Do you have a copy of it?

Mr. ROUSSELOT. I certainly do.

Mr. FLOOD. Then you go ahead and read it.

Mr. ROUSSELOT. I want the gentleman to read it to the whole House.

Mr. FLOOD. I read it. You read it.

Mr. ROUSSELOT. Is the gentleman still yielding?

Mr. FLOOD. Go ahead.

— Reps. John H. Rousselot (R-Calif.) and Daniel J. Flood (D-Pa.)
October 1, 1974

FLIGHT OF FANCY

Mr. D'AMATO. Senator, I have heard you on the floor before take this plane apart, hook by hook, piece by piece, and convince this body that the plan could not even fly.

Mr. GOLDWATER. You are out of your head.

Mr. D'AMATO. And you said it. I will read the record.

Mr. GOLDWATER. Read it. I never said that airplane would not fly.

Mr. D'AMATO. You said you would not fly it yourself.

Mr. GOLDWATER. I flew it.

Mr. D'AMATO. You said you would not, though, before you did.

Mr. GOLDWATER. I flew it.

Mr. D'AMATO. All right. Let me say this....

—Sens. Alfonse M. D'Amato (R-N.Y.) and Barry Goldwater (R-Ariz.)
October 16, 1986

x

DEPARTMENT
OF
AGRICULTURE

*Yes, sir,
pigs are smart*

DEPARTMENT
OF
AGRICULTURE

FELONIOUS FRUIT

Mr. CONTE. Now I would like to direct a question to my colleague from Massachusetts. As you know, I am a small farmer and maybe raise more tomatoes than anybody in this House.

The gentleman from Michigan (Mr. TRAXLER) has sampled and tasted some of my fine products.

Now this year I had an overabundance of tomatoes up there and I was away during the August recess so I, trying to be a decent neighbor, gave all of my neighbors on Lamar Road some of those surplus tomatoes. Now if I were under that marketing order, would I have been prohibited from doing that?

Mr. FRANK. Mr. Chairman, will the gentleman yield?

Mr. CONTE. I yield to my colleague from Massachusetts.

Mr. FRANK. I thank the gentleman for yielding.

I would say to my friend that I am glad that he speaks here under congressional immunity because I treasure my colleagues despite our partisan differences and he may have just committed a Federal crime or admitted to the commission of a crime by wantonly distributing tomatoes in violation of a marketing order and, yes, the imprudent distribution of food without the permission of the growers—and I want to say to the gentleman from Texas, if I can, I appreciate the fact that all these growers take time from their busy schedules of picking and planting and shaking and whatever, and they sit down and they have all these votes and they spend all this money just to benefit the consumer. It is an unparalleled example of beneficence. They are not looking, he tells us, to increase their income. It is solely to protect the consumer that they do all this work.

I would say to the gentleman from Massachusetts (Mr. CONTE) that those people who are doing all this work to help the consumer, shame on him for scattering those tomatoes in their way.

Mr. CONTE. Oh, thank you, thank you, thank you for sparing me from violating the law again.

Mr. TRAXLER. Mr. Chairman, will the gentleman yield?

Mr. CONTE. I yield to my colleague from Michigan.

Mr. TRAXLER. I thank the gentleman for yielding.

Mr. Chairman, my distinguished friend from Massachusetts is a fine tomato. I want to give some testimony here on his behalf and say that those tomatoes are some of the finest grown in the United States, even though they probably are illegal.

> — *Reps. Silvio O. Conte (R-Mass.), Barney Frank (D-Mass.), and*
> *Bob Traxler (D-Mich.)*
> *October 27, 1983*

GRAIN EXPECTATIONS

Mr. MATHIS. This bill, as I have said a number of times, is a compromise position between those people who want to destroy the program altogether and those people who want to hold onto what they have. I would submit that the gentleman from California probably really does not have the sentiments of his rice farmers in mind when he says he wants to destroy the program totally.

Mr. SYMMS. I thank the gentleman very much. I would like to assure the gentleman that it is not my intention to ever have this country become short of rice, because, as much as I like potatoes, and in Idaho we do like potatoes, I would hate to see them come to the point where they would have to throw potatoes at weddings.

> — *Reps. Dawson Mathis (D-Ga.) and Steven D. Symms (R-Idaho)*
> *December 10, 1975*

MEATING OF THE MINDS

Mr. CONTE. Mr. Chairman, I rise to assure my colleagues that I would not "steer" them wrong, but I must "raise a beef" about this bill.

This "choice" legislation is a "prime" example of what can make Congress "stew in its own juices."

It drips with excess "fat," while it "strips" the consumer.

This "beef-doggle" would raise retail meat prices by $60 million a year. No matter how you "slice" it, consumers are having their "flanks" attacked. They are being "slaughtered."

It was not my intent to "roast" the sponsors of this "bum steer." But I must remind them that consumers have a "stake" here too. But if this bill is "herded" through the House, many consumers will no longer have "steak."

You have all heard of Britain's "Rump Parliament" under Lord Cromwell. I fear that if this private interest bill for the beef industry passes, history will hereafter refer to us as the "Rump-Roast Congress."

I ask my colleagues to take this "bull by the horns," kill this bill, cut the fat off the bone, and "render" it back to the committee. It "butchers" lean consumer pocketbooks, and makes "mincemeat" of fiscal responsibility.

While I do not want to "rib" my friends from the cattle-raising States, I think that someone is trying to "pull the cowhide over our eyes."

I urge my colleagues to reject this "hunk of fat." It bleeds the American consumer. And I do not know a "knock wurst" than that.

> — *Rep. Silvio O. Conte (R-Mass.)*
> *October 2, 1975*

HOG WILD

Mr. SCHWENGEL. Mr. Speaker, I arise to set the record straight in a matter of very great importance to the constituents of my district, to Iowa, and this country.... My purpose here today, is to set the record straight with respect to the pork industry and the maligned pig....

I like pigs, and I honestly believe that most pigs like me. Hogs are beautiful. Some of my best friends are hogs....

To amuse ourselves, let us take a look at some of the uncomplimentary terms and phrases being heaped upon the poor pig. Consider these image-makers, for example:

She is *pigheaded.*
Her apartment is as dirty as a *pigsty.*
On weekends, she goes *hog wild.*
She knows as much about politics as a *hog* knows about Sunday.
She is always *hogging* the show.
What's more, she is a *road hog.*
Her Congressman is nothing but a *pork-barrel* politician who feeds at the Government trough.
I've never met her, but they say she is as *fat as a pig.*
Who wants to buy a *pig in the poke.*
Maybe she is all *lard,* who knows?
I've heard rumors that she casts her pearls before *swine.*
Does she have a cute little *piggy* bank?
Yes, I know, but you can't make a silk purse out of a *sow's ear.*
On the dance floor, she is as awkward as a *hog on ice.*

Now that we have a pig's eye image of this girl, how would you like to go whole hog and hire her as a member of your congressional staff?

So much for the scintillating semantics of swine slang. Now, I want to pay tribute to the noble pig for its 9,000 years of loyal service to mankind....

Yes, Sir; pigs are versatile creatures—and smart, too. Sometimes they are smarter than we think. For example, I recall a story I heard as a boy on my father's farm in Franklin County, Iowa, about the city slicker from Boston who bought a farm near ours. He wanted to get rich quick raising hogs. For a start he had one sow. He wanted some baby pigs so he loaded his sow into the wheelbarrow and pushed her up the road a couple of miles to the nearest neighbor to visit a boar. Then he wheeled the sow home again. Next morning he went to the barn bright and early, but to his surprise there were no little pigs. So he hoisted the sow into the wheelbarrow and repeated the journey. Next morning he went to the barn again—and still no little pigs. But there was the sow sitting in the wheelbarrow.

Yes, sir; pigs are smart....

— *Rep. Frederick D. Schwengel (R-Iowa)*
April 22, 1969

FRUIT SALAD

Mr. KELLY. Mr. Speaker, it is with reluctance I oppose and expose a plot among four very respected members of this House—Mr. ROBINSON of Virginia, Mr. McCORMACK of Washington, Mr. GOODLING of Pennsylvania, and Mr. SYMMS of Idaho. Apples are grown in their states.

And these men are out to upset our apple carts. Their recent actions show they want the whole bite of the apple for their constituents. They are part of the Big Apple cartel.

They have introduced a resolution naming the apple The Official Bicentennial Fruit and will ask this House to approve it. Their motives are exclusionary and certainly contrary to the spirit of the Revolution.

They trample on the customs of this venerable House, Mr. Speaker. They count apples and forget to tell us apples cannot be compared with oranges. I am here to say very little can compare with oranges....

To officially make the munching of an apple an act of patriotism is serious business.

It will change our American way of life, Mr. Speaker. They are meddling.

They could have all Hawaii's pineapple growers on the dole.

Things would no longer be peaches and cream in Georgia.

They might even try to declare life is nothing but a bowl of apples.

These comments are not sour grapes, my fellow Members of California and New York, but recognition of a clear and present danger. Their plotting is going to get us into a jam, a pickle.

These men imply apples were the first fruit brought to these shores. They claim America and apples are synonymous and that apples are the most popular and widely grown fruit in the United States.

All of that is so much applesauce....

I tell you, this power play by the Big Apple interests is rotten to the core.

Who, among the great orators in this House, ever speaks in apple-shaped tones? Who would feel comfortable with apples jubilee? Could anyone be so unaware of our heritage as to ask Billy Boy if she can bake an apple pie? Would many be so untraditional as to set a Thanksgiving table without cranberry sauce?

A popular variety of orange is the Parson Brown, Mr. Speaker. It is sweet to the palate and refreshing to the soul. Now, I ask you, what is more American than the name Parson Brown? Or just roll the word Valencia off your tongue. It makes you feel majestic to say it. It is an orange. Winesap is harsh to the ear. It is an apple.

Our orange blossom is the symbol of newlywed bliss. All the Big Apples have to offer is a song, "Don't Sit Under the Apple Tree With Anyone Else But Me," which is a wartime plea for fidelity. Are they trying to lead this Nation further down the road of permissiveness? Surely all of us recall what Eve started with the apple.

True, the apple has wormed its way into our folklore—things tend to be in apple pie order and as American as apple pie.

But the apple has had good public relations since the days of Johnny Appleseed. They want you to forget one rotten apple spoils the barrel.

And it may be true an apple a day keeps the doctor away. But have you every heard of anyone suffering the green apricot trots? Only apples can do that for you.

They keep quiet what Herman Melville said in his masterwork, Moby Dick: "Hell is an idea first born on an undigested apple dumpling."

Rather than give us full disclosure, they lull us with endearments: "apple of my eye" and "sweeter than apple cider"....

I sincerely hope my well-intended remarks do not earn me the reputation of being antiapple. I extend the olive branch. The apple is a noble fruit. I like it. I have them in my home. They are among the good things in life. They were of great importance in the settlement of this country. But just as the Nation had many Founding Fathers, it had many founding fruits.

But these men have shown they don't care a fig for the rest of us. As sure as God made little green apples, the sponsors of this resolution are about to offend the spirit that made America what it is today.

More fitting, Mr. Speaker, would be a resolution declaring the fruit salad our Bicentennial Appetizer. It would encourage dietary patriotism, in the interest of national unity, while avoiding potential widespread agricultural unemployment.

I believe this discourse has gone to the meat of the coconut. Let us do not buy a lemon. Let us preserve ourselves. Let us remember how our gardens grow.

—Rep. Richard Kelly (R-Fla.)
February 17, 1976

NUTS

Mr. CONTE. Mr. Chairman, I offer an amendment.
The Clerk read as follows:

Amendment offered by Mr. CONTE: Page 2, after line 25, add this new section:

"(c) Notwithstanding the provisions of section 301 of this Act or common sense, the Secretary shall make available to producers loans and purchases on the 1975 crop of fruit nuts at such levels as reflect the historical average relationship of fruit nut support levels to dingleberry support levels during the immediately preceding one hundred and ninety-nine years"...

Mr. Chairman, I rise to offer this amendment to this bill, an amendment entirely consistent with the principles and goals of H.R. 4296.

From this bill, I gather that it is now congressional style to propose drastic legislation without holding hearings, establish subsidy programs that were never asked for, and puff up price support levels so that big corporate farmers will be forever guaranteed fat annual profits.

My opinion of H.R. 4296 is this: Nuts!

It salts the consumer and will leave the farmer holding an empty shell.

To get into the nutty spirit of this bill, my amendment would establish a new subsidy program. It would be modeled exactly after the cotton program that the House is bailing out today. I am sure the characteristics will be familiar to all of you. My subsidy program will rip off the consumer, raid the Federal Treasury, provide incentives for overproduction, create massive surpluses, and necessitate future legislation establishing export subsidies and even higher price support levels.

The title of my new program is: "Subsidies for nuts."

Of course, I am serious about this. Do you think farm subsidies grow on trees?

The Agriculture Committee has acted as though that were true for years. My amendment is as nutty as the rest of the bill, so no one can truthfully say my amendment is not germane.

Are subsidies for nuts really necessary? After studying the cotton section of this bill, the only possible answer to that question is "Yes." Subsidies are the only way known to guarantee continued overproduction of a crop nobody needs. As far as this Congress is concerned, you just cannot have enough nuts around....

Let me explain how the loan program would work. I have modeled it after the cotton loan program. So it will be a nonrecourse loan. That means it does not have to be paid back. In fact, loans for nuts would not be repaid unless the market price for nuts rose above the Federal loan price. Of course, we would set the target price and loan-level price far above the presently depressed price for nuts. While this might destroy our competitive edge in foreign markets, it would warm our national prestige to have the world's highest priced nuts.

So, farmers like me could get big loans at the beginning of the crop year, and at the end of the year we could say nuts to the collateral and the loan, keep the money, and send the product to Washington. In other words, I could grow subsidies on trees and send my nuts to Butz....

Mr. Chairman, this amendment is germane because it is as nutty as the rest of the bill. I would advise all the taxpayers to hold on to their nuts because they are going to be worth a lot of money some day.

Mr. SYMMS. Mr. Chairman, will the gentleman yield so that I may ask him a question?

Mr. CONTE. I yield to the gentleman from Idaho.

Mr. SYMMS. Mr. Chairman, I would just like to ask the gentleman from Massachusetts if this amendment would affect nuts that are vended on the Penn Central Railroad which he supports so vociferously, for Government aid.

Mr. CONTE. I appreciate the gentleman's concern, and I want to assure him that if my amendment is passed it would put the nuts market in the same shape as the Penn Central.

—Reps. Silvio O. Conte (R-Mass.) and Steven D. Symms (R-Idaho)
March 20, 1975

OF ESP AND OTHER EARTHY SUBJECTS

Mr. PERCY. Mr. President, will the Senator yield at an appropriate point for a question?

Mr. HANSEN. I am happy to yield.

Mr. PERCY. Senator CULVER began his colloquy on the question of whether or not we can define what prime farmland is. I just wonder whether the Senator from Wyoming can now go back to his constituents and feel properly equipped to define and explain what primary farmland is.

Mr. HANSEN. The Senator uses the word "primary" as I understood him. He means "prime," does he not?

Mr. PERCY. That is correct, prime farmland.

Mr. HANSEN. A very simple answer to the Senator's question is, no, I could not.

Mr. PERCY. May this Senator put it in very simple terms, then, so my distinguished colleague could go back to his State and explain it? It is soils having aquic or udic moisture regimes; or soils having xeric or ustic moisture regimes.

If the farmer does not understand that, we could say soils having aridic or torric moisture regimes. If we want to be more specific, we could say soils have a soil temperature regime that is frigid, mesic, thermic, or hyperthermic—that is, pergelic or cryic regimes are excluded; or, soils with zero horizon which is higher than 47° Fahrenheit or 8° Centigrade.

If the farmer wants to have further explanation, I would go on to tell him then, as an expert in the field, that soils having a pH between 4.5 and 8.4 in all horizons within a depth of 40 inches would qualify, or that the conductivity of saturation extract that is less than 4 mmhos/cm and the exchangeable sodium percentage—that is, ESP—is less than 15....

Mr. HANSEN. Mr. President, I appreciate the always generous impulses of my good friend from Illinois....

I have to say that I do not propose to go out to Wyoming and respond to a question of what is prime farmland using some of this language. I am afraid I might get socked in the nose. They might misunderstand what I am trying to say when I use the words the Senator pronounces so easily and which I am afraid I would stumble over. They might even think I am calling them a bad name.

—Sens. Charles Percy (R-Ill.) and Clifford P. Hansen (R-Wyo.)
May 20, 1977

A FEW
TRIBUTES
FLOWERY
AND
OTHERWISE

*The Congress that
praises together . . .*

A FEW
TRIBUTES
FLOWERY
AND
OTHERWISE

NEVER THE TWAIN SHALL MEET

Mr. CANNON. Mr. Speaker, the repeal of this unnecessary and inequitable tariff on pipestems for corncob pipes further reduces the price of the components of this indispensable adjunct to human happiness.

Mr. Speaker, when the earliest pioneers from Virginia and the Carolinas first migrated to the motherly bosom of Missouri a century and a half ago, each settler brought with him his rifle, his Bible, and his pipe, and was equally proficient in the use of all three.

There on the fertile alluvial Mississippi and Missouri River bottoms and the rich loam of the Missouri uplands he found Indian maize yielding corn with cobs of such durable texture and generous proportions that he abandoned the colonial clay and briar bowls of the Old Dominion and adopted the Missouri meerschaum, which has become today the standard of pipe comfort, luxury, simplicity, economy, and enjoyment throughout the world.

Whether in London, or Shanghai, or San Francisco Bay, or the sidewalks of New York, buy a pipe at the nearest tobacconist's, and on the bottom of it you will read "Made in Missouri."

Fill it up with the golden flakes of your favorite smoke, preferably old homespun from a Missouri hillside, aged and ripened and mellowed in the top rafters of an ancient log tobacco barn, and it will give you such joy and solace as it is seldom human privilege to enjoy.

Mr. Speaker, I have placed an assortment of this exceptional product of Missouri's soil and industry in the cloakroom, and shall be glad to have the members of the House avail themselves of the opportunity to sample one of them. When you get crosswise with life, or digestion is bad; when things go wrong and you want to kick the dog; when the wife is critical and your best friends are out of town, tamp down an extra-heavy charge in one of these friendly pipes and light it with a coal from the fireplace, and peace and contentment will attend you like a benediction. Cares will vanish in dissolving rings of fragrant blue, and life once more will be worth the living.

—Rep. Clarence Cannon (D-Mo.)
July 2, 1960

WHERE THERE'S A WILL

Mr. BYRD. Will the Senator yield?

Mr. PROXMIRE. I yield.

Mr. BYRD. Words fitly spoken are like apples of gold in pictures of silver. I thank the distinguished Senator for his kind and overly charitable remarks. They have given me the tonic that I need for this long day.

Mr. PROXMIRE. I thank my good friend from West Virginia. With the possible exception of George Will, nobody can come up with these quotations better than the minority leader.

—Sens. Robert C. Byrd (D-W. Va.) and William Proxmire (D-Wis.)
September 27, 1986

A NATIONAL FLOWER

Mr. ALLOTT. Mr. President, in this hallowed Chamber, we are approaching a somewhat weedy situation. Various proposals for designation of our national flower are springing forth like shoots after a wet spring. They threaten to overrun other, even more vital issues.

I have nothing but the deepest of respect for my midwestern friends who champion the corn tassel. There is no great personal objection on my part to the reproductive significance of this fertile portion of that grand vegetable. Nor do I disdain the grass on which we walk, and which others would have us call our "flower."

My admiration for the good taste of the advocates of the rose is equally great. I grow the flower in my own garden at home. Like so many others, I have been injured by its thorns; but I bear the flower no malice.

However, for our national floral emblem, all these proposals suffer from distinct blights. Two are not true flowers in the accepted sense. The third is the national flower of five other nations, against one of which our forefathers fought—and in that conflict so many died—to gain our country's freedom.

Therefore, I propose as our national flower, a true flower, one which is the most widely grown cut flower in the United States, one which is perpetually flowering and knows no season. I present it in the spirit of Webster, Clay, and Calhoun, the spirit of amicable compromise. I offer for your consideration, Mr. President: The carnation.

Here is a flower acceptable to and appropriate for men as well as for women. Yet it has been accepted by former Congresses and Presidents as the official flower of Mother's Day.

The carnation is a true flower. It is grown and used only for its floral beauty and its symbolism. It has no problems, no thorns, no foliage dropoff, virtually no allergic effects....

In selecting something so beautiful as a national flower should be, let us cultivate the good which makes America. Let us not mock the flower or mimic other nations. Let us not quarrel over such matters. Let us unite behind the carnation. Let us resolve this floral dispute by forging the second "great compromise." ...

Mr. KEATING subsequently said: Mr. President, I wish to express my personal gratitude to the distinguished Senator from Colorado [Mr. ALLOTT] for sending to me today a carnation to wear.

However, I invite his attention to a fact with respect to which he may not be informed, regarding the proudest, oldest, and loveliest flower—the rose. I invite his attention to the fact that fossils of the genus rosa, establishing the existence of the rose on this continent for more than 33 million years—considerably longer than this body has been in existence—were found in his own native state of Colorado. It is possible that this horticultural fact has escaped the attention of the Senator from Colorado, and that upon realization of that fact he may feel that Colorado should join the State of New York, which has made the rose its State flower. I sincerely hope that that will be the effect of my remarks today....

Mr. DIRKSEN. Mr. President, will the Senator from New York yield to me?

Mr. KEATING. I yield to the Senator from Illinois.

Mr. DIRKSEN. Of course, English history records the War of the Roses, between the House of York and the House of Lancaster. I hope, after this long interlude, that the War of the Roses will not be resumed.

Mr. HICKENLOOPER. Mr. President, I am distressed to hear what I consider to be the misguided arguments being advanced here today.

The idea of a national flower or a national floral emblem is highly desirable, but I invite attention to the fact that some of us have introduced a bill proposing that the corn tassel be the national flower. With all respect to my friend from Colorado and my friend from New York, one of whom advocates the carnation and the other the rose, the corn tassel has various attributes. Corn has varied and diverse uses. One can speculate indefinitely on the use of corn in many ways. The corn tassel is a very beautiful flower. It represents food, among other things. It represents the strength of our country. It represents the hope of our agricultural regions—and all States are agricultural.

It seems to me that it is not only decorative, but it has great utility, which should appeal. While the rose is beautiful, and is grown in all States, and while the carnation is a wonderful flower, and has great sentimental value, being seen in profusion at funerals, and while I would not discredit the beauty of those flowers, I importune my colleagues to think about the stability and utility of corn, as represented by the corn tassel.

Mr. KEATING. I do not intend to express opposition to corn.

Mr. NEUBERGER. Mr. President, I should like to point out to my colleagues on the other side of the aisle that more roses grow in Oregon than in any other State, and that, unlike the corn tassel, the rose does not need price supports to enable it to flourish. [Laughter.]

Mr. MORTON subsequently said: Mr. President, I regret that I was necessarily absent during the early part of the morning hour because of an engagement I had in downtown Washington. I wish I had been present on the floor at the time my colleague from Colorado introduced his joint resolution designating the carnation as the national flower of the United States.

Mr. President, I wear a carnation. I might add it was given to me, free. I bear the carnation no malice. It is a beautiful flower. From the esthetic standpoint, it serves as a thing of beauty. I have not been able to find that it makes any great contribution to the welfare of our Nation or that it is essential to our economic survival in this troubled world.

I understand, too, that the corn tassel came up for more discussion this morning as a proposed national flower. May I point out that the corn tassel is not a full flower. It is merely the male flower. The ear of the corn is the female flower of the corn plant. I do not think we want to get into any controversy that is going to lose us the women's vote because of our adopting a male flower as the national floral emblem.

I might add, incidentally, that corn is converted into various products. Some of this conversion takes place in my native State of Kentucky. I know from experience we do not want to get into a debate, on what should be the national flower, that is going to stir up the Anti-Saloon League.

I again bring forth the proposal I made some time ago. At the appropriate time I shall introduce the proper resolution. It is that grass be our national flower.

There are those who say grass is not a flower, but I point out that grass does flower and seed. I point out that our first important resource is grass, and that our most important resource is the cow. Let us look at the cow, the foster mother of mankind. Where would the cow be, and, further, where would mankind be, but for grass? We are a meat-eating people. How could we satisfy our national hunger for meat, if it were not for grass, on which feed the animals that supply us with beef and mutton and lamb in such lavish quantities....

Mr. DOUGLAS. I will say to the Senator from Kentucky, a large part of the prosperity of Kentucky has been built upon corn, also—corn put into a liquid form. It is corn which perhaps should not have been imbibed by the people of this country, but nevertheless it is taken in a liquid form.

It ill behooves the Senator from Kentucky to try to upgrade grass and downgrade corn.

Mr. MORTON. Mr. President, will the Senator yield?

Mr. DOUGLAS. I yield.

Mr. MORTON. I want to make clear I was not trying to ridicule the Senator's resolution. I know the Senator is serious and is perfectly sincere in his objective.

As I pointed out earlier, there are some difficulties which I foresee in the legislative path with regard to the adoption of a national flower, as we go through the long legislative process of providing law.

I considered the case of corn, and I pointed out that the corn tassel is the male part of the flower and is not the full flower. The Senator will find Susan B. Anthony rolling over in her grave, should he make the fight for the corn tassel.

With respect to the Senator's remarks regarding the contribution of corn in my own State, the Senator will find the Anti-Saloon League and the WCTU knocking on his door to say, "Down with the corn tassel."

I merely bring out the point that the road before the Senator is a hard and rough road. I wish him well, but I intend to continue the fight for grass....

—*Sens. Gordon L. Allott (R-Colo.), Kenneth B. Keating (R-N.Y.), Everett M. Dirksen (R-Ill.), Bourke B. Hickenlooper (R-Iowa), Richard L. Neuberger (D-Ore.), and Paul H. Douglas (D-Ill.) February 26, 1959*

BET ON THE OSTRICH

Mrs. SCHROEDER. Mr. Speaker, during the past 2 weeks, a Member of this body, whose ornithological knowledge is as sadly deficient as his courtesy, heaped undeserved insult on the ostrich, not to mention on his colleagues.

He described as "ostriches" his Republican and Democratic colleagues who opposed President Reagan's Nicaragua policies.

One would hope that the merits of U.S. policies in Central America could be discussed without insulting birds or colleagues.

Over the millenia, the ostrich developed defensive and offensive capabilities that enabled it to survive in lands where lions and other carnivorous predators abounded. It runs at high speeds—up to 40 miles an hour—and if riled or cornered, can deliver a vicious, lethal kick.

With large eyes and keen vision, the ostrich is ever alert. Contrary to myth, the ostrich does not stick its head in the sand. Nor does it spend much time booming at C-SPAN cameras in an empty Chamber. When necessary, it lies on the ground as a means of camouflage.

Finally, it has simple needs, grazing mainly on plants and capable of going without water for long periods of time.

So there you have it. The ostrich is a rugged, wiley, and frugal bird. Indeed, in a scrap between the Member of Congress and an ostrich, I would bet on the ostrich.

—Rep. Patricia Schroeder (D-Colo.)
April 24, 1985

ALOHA

Mr. FORD. Mr. President, will the distinguished Senator from Hawaii yield for a question since he has the floor?

Mr. MATSUNAGA. I am happy to yield for a question or for a statement.

Mr. FORD. Is one of the attractions of Hawaii the weather?

Mr. MATSUNAGA. Yes.

Mr. FORD. Once you get on the island you cannot get off, so you do not need billboards.

[Laughter.] ...

Mr. MATSUNAGA. I must say in response to the Senator from Kentucky that if he has not yet been to Hawaii, may I ask whether he has visited Hawaii or not?

Mr. FORD. I say to the distinguished Senator from Hawaii, yes, I have been to Honolulu, I have been to the big island. I understand Parker Ranch. Yes, I do, and I was at Kona at the motel.

Mr. MATSUNAGA. I am glad the Senator from Kentucky has been there because now that he has been there he knows what Heaven looks like. And if on Judgment Day he is directed to go the other way, at least he will have that satisfaction.

[Laughter.]

—Sens. Wendell H. Ford (D-Ky.) and Spark M. Matsunaga (D-Hawaii)
February 3, 1987

THE CHARM OF QUARKS

And other golden fleeces

THE
CHARM
OF
QUARKS

ARE YOU LISTENING, IDI?

Mr. DERWINSKI. Mr. Speaker, Cicero called Aristotle a river of flowing gold. If Cicero were alive and operating in the Nation's Capital, he unquestionably would discover a rich golden alternative to Aristotle. It is the National Endowment for the Humanities.

Obviously and forensically, I make no attempt to speak for Cicero, but I rather imagine he would have laughed all the way to the Forum, if he could have foreseen that his B.C. wit would be the subject of a 20th-century Federal grant. Fortunately or unfortunately, depending upon your point of view, we soon may have some definitive answers from the French Department of the University of Illinois. The department has been awarded a grant of up to $22,000 to provide a fellowship for the study of Cicero's jokes in Renaissance France and Italy. I wonder if the joke is not really on us.

Of course, if we have any reservations about coming out on the short end of that deal the National Endowment for the Humanities already is a step ahead of us. It has awarded a $22,000 outright grant for a fellowship which will concentrate on "Origins of the Doctrine of Unequal Exchange."

I must confess to a sentimental interest in another $22,000 outright grant. It was awarded for a fellowship which will study "The Folk Rituals of Birth, Marriage and Death Among Urban Polish-Americans."

In reviewing the recent list of grants approved by the National Endowment for the Humanities, I was left with a song in my heart. It was indeed heart warming to learn another grant of up to $22,000 will be available for a fellowship which will focus on "An Ethnomusicological Study of the Harp Traditions of Uganda."

Are you listening, Idi Amin, wherever you are?

— Rep. Edward J. Derwinski (R-Ill.)
January 30, 1981

STARK DIFFERENCES

Mr. STARK. Mr. Speaker, the Washington Post reports that the Army has granted a $139,000 contract to the University of Maryland to conduct a study of how to prepare healthy food that tastes good. I submit that the Army asking a college food service about healthy, tasty food is rather like Phyllis Diller asking Joan Rivers about beauty aids....

— Rep. Fortney H. (Pete) Stark (D-Calif.)
October 10, 1986

SOUR PUSS

Mr. GROSS. In the absence of the gentleman from New York (Mr. ROONEY) I would like to ask the gentleman from Michigan (Mr. CEDERBERG) if he feels that the $1,300,000 contained in the bill for lemonade will be sufficient for the State Department for next year.

Mr. CEDERBERG. There are some who think it will not be sufficient. I think it will. The price of lemonade, as I understand it, has increased quite substantially due to the devaluation of the dollar abroad. I trust they have not had any freeze in the lemon trees out in California. I do not know whether they have not, but I think the $1,300,000 is adequate.

I told the gentleman from Iowa earlier that after the gentleman retires, if he takes a trip abroad, we want him to get special treatment when he goes into some of these other countries so that he can find out for himself whether or not we are properly handling this kind of a situation.

Mr. GROSS. It would be my hope, Mr. Chairman, if the gentleman would yield further, that by the time I go abroad that Congress would have abolished the representation allowance—I believe it is still called that, although it is sometimes called the booze and food allowance for the State Department.

Mr. CEDERBERG. Yes, hope always springs eternal, but I would not count on it.

Mr. GROSS. I thank the gentleman for his solicitude, if and when I should go abroad.

— Reps. H.R. Gross (R-Iowa) and Elford A. Cederberg (R-Mich.)
June 18, 1974

ST. NIX

Mr. SYMMS. Mr. Speaker, rumors are flying around Washington to the effect that this may have been Santa Claus' last year of operation. Sources within the federal bureaucracy are privately indicating that the jolly old man is in big, big trouble.

Apparently, from the Federal Government's point of view, Santa has been "getting away with murder" for years now, "breaking every law in the book," as they put it. And indeed, the time has come to crack down on this unconscionable situation.

Here is the inside scoop on Santa's long list of infractions:

First. Operating a flying sleigh in absence of certification by the CAB, a clear violation of the Civil Aeronautics Act of 1938.

Second. Unlawfully competing with the U.S. Postal Service on air mail deliveries.

Third. Violating EPA requirements for emissions control devices on his reindeer.

Fourth. Breaking the Sherman Antitrust Act by maintaining a strict monopoly in his profession.

Fifth. Violating the Fair Labor Standards Act by failing to pay his elves the minimum wage or proper overtime benefits.

Sixth. Engaging in unfair promotional advertising, designed to prey on the defenseless minds of children, a violation of Federal Trade Commission regulations.

Seventh. Failing to secure an ICC permit and an assignment of certified routes by the Interstate Commerce Commission.

Eighth. Violating numerous Occupational Safety and Health Administration—OSHA—regulations by operating an "unsafe workplace."

Ninth. Passing out candy canes and goodies not approved by the Food and Drug Administration.

Tenth. Ignoring the edicts of the Equal Employment Opportunity Commission and the Civil Rights Act of 1964 by failing to institute a quota system in his workshop based on race, religion, sex, and size—too many elves.

Eleventh. Making toys which were not approved by the Consumer Product Safety Commission.

Twelfth. Failing to declare the cookies and milk which are out for him as taxable income with the IRS.

Thirteenth. Transporting firearms across State lines as Christmas presents.

Fourteenth. Avoiding State and Federal taxes on his sleigh, not to mention licensing, registration, and having an operator's permit.

Fifteenth. Making various infractions of National Labor Relations Board regulations; including the maintenance of a nonunion shop and unfairly competing with the chimney sweeps' union.

Mr. Speaker, it is said that these are but a sampling of Santa's more serious Federal offenses, which taken in total, will almost certainly put the man in red out of business for good.

—*Rep. Steven D. Symms (R-Idaho)*
December 20, 1974

THE CHARM OF QUARKS

Mr. BELLMON. Mr. President, I wish to share with my colleagues the excitement members of the Appropriations Subcommittee on Public Works felt the other day as a result of the testimony about the accomplishments of the Department of Energy's (DOE) Office of Energy Research. A portion of the testimony of Dr. John M. Deutch, Director of the Office of Energy Research, follows:

ACCOMPLISHMENTS

This is a time of great discovery and exploration especially in the realm of the quark. The excitement and promise in high energy physics haven't been as great since the 1950's. Phenomena displaying the explicit properties of charm have been revealed through the copious production of the D mesons at SLAC—as opposed to the hidden charm that is characteristic of the J/Psi particles. The confidence in the quark concept was further extended this past year by the discovery at Fermilab of the upsilon particle, and ultra-heavy member analogous to the J/Psi particles but at about three times the mass of the J/Psi (ten times the mass of the proton). Just as the J/Psi signaled the existence of the fourth (charmed) quark, the upsilon is believed to be the first evidence of a fifth type of quark. Much excitement attends confirmation of this result and the search for new particles carrying the fifth quark.

There has also been substantial progress in other areas of study. There is considerable evidence now that heavy leptons, beyond the muon, are a reality....

Mr. BELLMON. I doubt that any of you who were not there can imagine the excitement this testimony engendered in the hearts of the members of the committee. This excitement was produced at a total budget outlay in fiscal year 1978 of about a half-billion dollars. The requested appropriations for the Office of Energy Research in fiscal year 1979 is $618 million and that does not include about $250 million more than is being asked for a machine called Isabelle. When Isabelle begins relating symbiotically with SLAC and ZGS, and Dr. Deutch gets cooking with his half-billion dollars, can a solution to the energy problem be far off?

There are two things wrong with the kind of testimony this DOE official has presented to our committee. That testimony is supposed to persuade us Senators that we should appropriate the money requested. Well, not only am I not persuaded by the testimony; I do not even understand it. For me, the charm of quarks is well hidden....

—Sen. Henry L. Bellmon (R-Okla.)
March 21, 1978

SPITTING IMAGES

Mr. COX. Let any member go through the corridors of the Departments and look in the open doors; and, except the women who work faithfully, he will find a good many clerks, when not engaged in reading newspapers, talking politics and spitting tobacco-juice. There is no man in all the world like an American clerk for splendid spitting. There never were clerks or persons who could excel them in the flux of their salivary glands! [Laughter.] No country, sir, rejoices in such great prairies, wonderful rivers, large lakes, high mountains, and such a great people as our own beloved land; but in one thing, sir, we surpass the world and ourselves. Our American clerks can spit higher, spit farther, and spit more than any other people on the face of the earth—and get more pay for the performance! I still except the women clerks as to this salivary performance.

—Rep. Samuel Cox (D-N.Y.)
May 8, 1879

ALL HANDS OFF DECKS

Mr. PROXMIRE. Mr. President, I am awarding my Golden Fleece of the Month Award for March to the Department of the Air Force for decking taxpayers about $59,000 over the last 6 years for the cost of playing cards that were given away as souvenirs to visitors aboard Air Force Two. Technically, the Air Force gets the Fleece because they spent the money, but the blame should be shared by the Executive Office of the President, which usually makes these requests.

In this day and time of outrageous Federal spending, we certainly do not need to have taxpayers subsidizing poker and gin rummy for guests who fly on the official Vice Presidential plane.

It looks like the taxpayers have been dealt another bad hand. This is a classic case. We've got a Joker of a Federal budget deficit that needs to be Aced soon, or we'll all go busted. But here we are throwing away tens of thousands of dollars in hard-earned tax money to buy playing cards for the Vice Presidential aircraft. It makes no sense. I think the Executive Office has drawn a bum card on this one.

The Air Force explains this fanciful flight into financial frenzy by saying that these playing cards are for official use. Only the Vice President and his staff are authorized to distribute them. And these are not just any old playing cards. They are inscribed with the Vice Presidential seal and all sorts of other trim. These cards may make nice memorabilia, but their importance in terms of the national interest escapes me. The taxpayer may question who is playing with a full deck on this one....

For now, this year's version of the "Zap the Taxpayers" card game appears to be on hold. The contract solicitation was suddenly canceled. According to the Air Force, the solicitation was pulled upon discovery that only one company was able to fulfill a special requirement to bronze the Vice Presidential seal. Now the more expensive bronzing requirement has been dropped, and the Air Force says another deal for the specially made decks may still be in the cards. They just don't know when to hold them and when to fold them.

When you take a look at the description the Air Force's Washington Area Contracting Center gave in seeking bids on this most unusual project, you'll know this was no ordinary set of playing cards:

> Cards, playing, single deck, bronzed with current Vice Presidential seal, "black on gold" on back of all cards . . . with "Welcome Aboard Air Force Two" printed in gold on back of all cards. Jokers to include image of capitol building on face, deck in light blue velour case * * * Vice Presidential seal in gold * * *

I have seen a lot of card tricks, but this one beats them all. This is one case where somebody needs to play a trump card for the taxpayers.

—Sen. William Proxmire (D-Wis.)
March 10, 1987

I THINK
THAT
I SHALL
NEVER
SEE

*Miscellaneous reports from the
Joint Committee on
Public Poesy*

I THINK
THAT
I SHALL
NEVER
SEE

OUR TEAM THE DUST DID BIT

Mr. CONTE. Mr. Speaker, my own words would be inadequate to describe the action on the diamond last evening as my mighty elephants tasted the unaccustomed bitterness of defeat at the hands of the Democratic team. Thus, I have borrowed the words of the great poet Coleridge, who so well portrayed the crushing weight of the Albatross we must wear around our necks until next year. I have dedicated this following poem to my great team, and have titled it "The Rime of the Ancient Manager."

I am an ancient manager
   And stoppeth one of thee.
"By thy bended back and mournful face,
   What canst thou say to me?"
I hold you with a tearful eye
   And tell of my defeat
At the hands of the rebel donkeys
   Whose victory was complete.

The sides are drawn, the game is on;
   My men are braced to score,
And LeBoutillier, with his arm's fair sway
   Tried to break their mighty corps.
Pitches, pitches, everywhere
   But not a ball to hit.
Pitches, pitches, everywhere
   Our team the dust did bit.

McCloskey was here, Fields was there,
   The plays were all around.

They fielded and caught, and hit and ran,
  Their feet fleet on the ground.

But Fauntroy fetched and Downey delivered
  When then the field they took,
While Oxley's bat and Cohen's crack
  Couldn't match that Mottl hook.

God save me—the ancient manager,
  From the fouls that plague me so!
An Albatross was easier hit
  Than an arrow from Mottl's bow!
Our failure last eve is not easy explained
  Or our low home run score yield—
We weren't idle as a painted team
  Upon a painted field.

We played our game as best they came
  And relished every play—
The elephants shall rise again
  And win another day!

Now I shall not belabor more
  This doleful manager's rime,
So save the tears and condolences
  Until they lose next time.

This manager hath now been stung
  And is of sense forlorn.
A sadder, but a wiser man
  He'll rise to face the morn.

— Rep. Silvio O. Conte (R-Mass.)
June 17, 1982

A FEW MINUTES TO KILL

Mr. GUYER. Mr. Chairman, I too would like to say a few good words about the gentleman from Illinois (Mr. DERWINSKI) but I just cannot think of any right now. However, I would like to say something about our chairman, the gentleman from Pennsylvania (Mr. MORGAN) because I think doctors are probably the most unappreciated people in the world. One the other day was so much of a failure that he turned to bank robbing and he was not very good at that, either, because every time he held a note up to the tellers, they could not read it.

But, Mr. Chairman, I would like to pay the gentleman from Pennsylvania, Dr. MORGAN, a little tribute since we have a few minutes to kill. I know it is getting late, but we do have time to use up. We usually talk by the yard, think by the inch and go out by the foot. I have a little poem I would like to quote:

A man stood at the Pearly Gate
His face was scarred and old,
He stood before that Man of Fate,
For admission to the fold.

"What have you done," the Angel said,
"To gain admission here?"
"I have been a hard-working committee chairman
For many and many a year."

The Pearly Gate swung open wide
The Angel touched the bell,
"Come in and choose your harp," he said
"You've had your share of Hell."

> — *Rep. Tennyson Guyer (R-Ohio)*
> *May 19, 1976*

GREAT SCOTT, SILVIO!—I

Mr. CHAPPELL. Mr. Speaker, I take this 1 minute to discuss briefly the ball game tomorrow night.

Silvio ... my Silvio ... I rise, to salute
Your Congressional Team (of dubious repute),
T'will cause me great anguish, great pain
To know that your ball team will journey, in vain.

To Four Mile Run Field—where they hadn't oughta,
The site of our game, the scene of your slaughter!
Silvio, my friend, in just two short days,
We'll take the field, our spirits ablaze!

Your Nine will not fall to some devious trick ...
But rather will feel the sting of our "kick"
And as, from that field, they carry your men,
We'll loan 'em Ace bandages and liniment, then.

You must know, Oh Silvio, respect you I do,
(And extol your prowess as a Congressman, too!)
But when "playing ball" is the pathway to fame,
Great Scott, Silvio! We, the Democrats, invented the game!

So send on your Chandler, Lungren, Kasich and Paul,
Oxley, Pursell and Fields—send 'em all!
For Williams, Schaefer, McKernan and Crane
Will all fall back ... in definite pain!!

You see, my dear Colleague, the trouble you're in,
Is that Democrats are taught, from childhood, to win!
But one fond hope, Silvio ... when that contest ends:
Promise me ... Paisan ... that we'll still be friends!

—Rep. Bill Chappell, Jr. (D-Fla.)
July 26, 1983

GREAT SCOTT, SILVIO!—II

Mr. CONTE. Mr. Speaker—

You know Caruso, Domingo, and Luke Pavarotti
All the great voices not nasty or naughty
But do you recall
The greatest Italian singer of all?

Take me out to the ball game
Take me out with the staff
Let me watch Russo fall on his face
Never will Chappell be so disgraced!
And I'll root, root, root for the G.O.P.
I know we'll recover our fame.
We've got a great pitcher who's never been beat.
Our hitters use pine tar but not on their feet
Our outfield eats fly balls like doggies eat meat.
And I know we'll win!

Come out tonight—Four Mile Run Stadium in Alexandria for the great annual face-off. Only $2.50 for the game, $7.50 for the game and the party before.

— Rep. Silvio O. Conte (R-Mass.)
July 27, 1983

GREAT SCOTT, SILVIO!—III

Mr. CONTE. Mr. Speaker—

Half a run, Half a run,
Half a run onward,
Out of the Dugout of Doom
Rose the mighty fourteen.
"Forward, Mighty Pachyderms!
Charge for the balls," I screamed:
Into the outfield of Death
Rode the mighty fourteen.

Theirs was not to catch the fly,
Theirs was not to tag Faunt-ry
Theirs was but to win, or tie
Back to the Dugout of Doom
Rode the mighty fourteen.

Pitchers to the right of them
Pitchers to the left of them

Pitchers right in front of them
Volleyed and beaned.

Oxley ran with might and fleet
Dan Crane's hits could not be beat
Into the jaws of victory
And out of the mouth of Defeat
Rode the mighty fourteen.

Flash! as Pursell leapt in air
Flash! as Schaefer's arm would scare
Striking out the batters fair
While Williams called the shots from there
And Chappell sat and steamed.
Ran out Ron Paul's fast ball's smoke
Through their outfield line we broke
Liberal and conservative
Reeled from that batter's stroke.
What a mighty team!
The donkeys they fell back, but not
Not the great fourteen.

Doubles to the left of them
Singles to the right of them
Triples far behind them
Volleyed and careened
Bonior's bat could feel the heat
Russo's strength was in his feet
With great pop flies by Alan Wheat
Dems, they sought the victory
From the mighty team
It would have to be hard won
From the great fourteen.

How could their great glory fade?
O, the errors that they made
A tie was unforeseen
Honor true the charge they made
Honor true our Might Brigade
Noble, great fourteen.

— *Rep. Silvio O. Conte (R-Mass.)*
July 28, 1983

DEBT AND TAXES

Mr. ASHLEY. Mr. Chairman, this is the first time that legislation to extend the excise tax on certain commodities and the corporate tax rate has been included in legislation to extend the temporary debt limit in a bill reported under a rule which permits no amendments....

A constituent has supplied the following poetic contribution as reflective of current taxpayer sentiment which I think we will do well to keep in mind:

There's tax when I phone and a tax when I wire.
There's a tax on my heat, and my fireplace fire.
There's tax on my lights and a tax on my books
And if I would fish, there's a tax on my hooks.
There's a tax on my hat and a tax on each shoe.
There's a tax on my shirt and other things, too.
There's a tax on the oil I rub on my hair
And a tax on the toothpaste I use with such care.
I am taxed if I gargle, and if I get ill
I'm taxed if I swallow a capsule or pill.
I'm taxed when I plan and taxed when I talk
And a tax on my sex makes me taxed when I walk.
They tax all the money I earn, beg, or win.
Then tax me aplenty for blowing it in.

— *Rep. Thomas L. Ashley (D-Ohio)*
June 8, 1960

A POET BY ANY OTHER NAME

Mr. HEFLIN. Mr. President, today we are considering a resolution which would designate the rose as our national floral emblem.

This resolution came before the Judiciary Committee last week, and I freely admit that I questioned it a bit. After all, our Nation can boast of a veritable cornucopia of beautiful flowers. For instance, my home State, Alabama, has chosen the camellia as its State flower. Also among the ranks of State flowers are the carnation, the flowering dogwood, the magnolia, the violet, the sunflower, and even mistletoe, among many others.

In fact, we have so many beautiful flowers that I even thought of suggesting to my colleagues on the Judiciary Committee, somewhat tongue in cheek, that, instead of a single national floral emblem, we designate a different flower for each day of the week. In that way, we could recognize at least seven different flowers for their unique qualities, by, for instance, designating the rose as the national flower of Sunday, the camellia as the national flower of Monday, and so on. Of course, in my heart, I knew this was an unworkable solution, even though one of my distinguished colleagues on the committee suggested that I was really looking for a national bouquet....

Mr. President, as you can see, during my consideration of this resolution, I have gone through a variety of thought processes. To symbolize this, and to tell the story of this resolution, along with Peck Fox of my staff and I have drafted a short poem.

Roses are red,
   Violets are blue,
Why must I choose
   Between these two?

Marigolds and dogwood,
   Camellias and more,
All flowers are beautiful
   And made to adore.

But today there are deficits,
   And farm bills and trade,
Aren't these the subjects
   On which decisions should be made?

Still, if on a Nation's flower
   A few moments we spend,
We might be refreshed and
   Come down to Earth again.

Besides, to select a flower
   As America's might not be bad,
Because we sure don't want
   To make the garden clubs mad.

But all flowers are delicate
   Each can refresh and amuse,
And that is the reason
   I feel no flower should lose.

Still the rose is universal,
   Its support has a strong voice,
So there should no question
   That the rose is the choice.

So let us raise our voices, and
   Proclaim with all our power
That the rose is more than beautiful—
   It is "America's Flower."

Mr. JOHNSTON. Mr. President, roses are red, violets are blue, HEFLIN should be a coauthor of this bill, too.

—Sens. Howell Heflin (D-Ala.) and J. Bennett Johnston (D-La.)
September 16, 1985

THE BARD FROM FARGO

Mr. BURDICK. I would like to conclude with the thoughts of one of my constituents, Mr. Bill Snyder, of Fargo, ND. Mr. Snyder dared me to include his poem in the CONGRESSIONAL RECORD. Well, here it goes, Mr. Snyder.

Chop the old folks,
Cut the young,
Slice the budget,
Rung by rung.
But never, never,
Vote away,
Any boost
In Congressman's pay!

—Sen. Quentin N. Burdick (D-N.D.)
January 29, 1987

THE DOG ATE MY HOMEWORK AND THE LORD UNDERSTANDS

Mrs. SCHROEDER. Mr. Speaker, I marvel at the President's ability to move around, visiting one function or another—Reagan/Bush rallies, Republican fundraisers, dinner with his penpal, a songfest at the Grand Ole Opry, and photo opportunities galore. If I had a dollar for every photo opportunity Reagan's offered, I could settle the national debt with a personal check.

During the Presidential debate Sunday evening Mr. Reagan excused himself from attending church because he is afraid of a terrorist attack. "I think the Lord understands," he explained. Fundraisers and rallies yes, but church services no. I'm sure the Lord is still trying to figure that one out....

So it is heartening to see that Reagan is expanding his repertory. He now has enough alibis, excuses, and absolutions for a full-scale Broadway musical.

We could call it, "The Dog Ate My Homework."

To paraphrase T.S. Eliot: He always has an alibi, and one or two to spare: At whatever time the deed took place—Reagan wasn't there.

> — *Rep. Patricia Schroeder (D-Colo.)*
> *October 10, 1984*

REID WRITES

Mr. REID. Mr. Speaker, for the amusement and edification of my colleagues, I am passing along a bit of the poetic wit and wisdom of Reid B. Gardner, a friend and constituent from Las Vegas, NV. Reid's words are fine/His rhymes sublime/Better than mine/Without further ado/Here's a sample for you:

Richard Nixon, in reflection
Wondered where he'd lost direction
In fame's forest, found that he
Had climbed up higher than his tree.

WILL THE GENTLEMAN YIELD?

I'm working hard for ERA
Tho I'm sure some will abuse it
My reasons are both strong and clear
We married men could use it.

The weather today, to be succinct
Didn't turn out the way I thinkt.

The early bird, he gets the worms
And feeds them to his mate
My wife was never fond of worms
So I just sleep in late.

The Hebrews wandered 40 years
Across the desert soil
They hunted manna every day
When they should have looked for oil.

— Rep. Harry Reid (D-Nev.)
April 29, 1985

HELLO, I MUST BE GOING

Blowhards, filibusterers, and other practitioners of the art of longwindedness

HELLO,
I MUST BE
GOING

FIVE, FOUR, THREE, TWO, ONE

Mr. MOYNIHAN. I see my distinguished friend, the chairman of the Budget Committee, has risen. If he would like me to yield for a question, I would be happy to do so.

Mr. DOMENICI. I would be delighted if you would yield for a question without losing your right to the floor.

Mr. MOYNIHAN. I am happy to do so.

Mr. DOMENICI. Provided you permit a bit of liberty. My question may be slightly lengthy, maybe not more than 3 or 4 minutes. Is that all right with the Senator?

Mr. MOYNIHAN. His remarks can scarcely be more lengthy than the continuing resolution.

Mr. DOMENICI. Let me just say this. I do not want the Senator from New York to answer this question, but I doubt very much if the U.S. Senate or the U.S. House, with or without Gramm-Rudman-Hollings, would add $30 billion to the defense budget. What are we talking about? Gramm-Rudman-Hollings cut the defense budget $320 billion over the President's request. That is absolutely incredible....

Mr. MOYNIHAN. I wonder if the Senator would tell me what his question is.

Mr. DOMENICI. My question will be here soon, I say to my friend from New York.

Now let me tell you something else, and we will put this one in the record. For those who think this year we are only cutting defense, let me tell you this is a phenomenal year....

Mr. MOYNIHAN. Could I ask my friend once again what is his question?

Mr. DOMENICI. It will get there. Thirty seconds. My distinguished leader asks that I ought to ask you what the time is.

Mr. MOYNIHAN. It is 30 seconds from the time you are going to stop talking. [Laughter.]

Mr. DOMENICI. Now I have another question. Let me just finish this. Let us talk about the next best year in terms of growth reduction in the Federal budget. You might have said it was 1981 that the revolution began. That is not right. You might have said it was 1982. That is not right. You might have said 1985....

Mr. MOYNIHAN. Five, four, three, two, one.

Mr. DOMENICI. All I had to say was I cannot believe anybody would seriously say we are in some kind of a jam over this trainer aircraft because of Gramm-Rudman-Hollings, unless they are prepared to say that we were really going to give the President everything in defense he has asked for....

Mr. MOYNIHAN. Mr. President, who has the floor?

> *—Sens. Pete V. Domenici (R-N.M.) and Daniel Patrick Moynihan (D-N.Y.)*
> *October 16, 1986*

NO SECRET

Mr. STEVENS. Now, God forbid that anyone will ever tell me that the city of Washington is my home; it is not. I detest it. I really do. I cannot think of another place to have a nation's capital in the world that is a worse place to live. The air compared to my State is abominable. We shorten our life spans by coming to this town. As far as I am concerned, I know of no town—no town—that has a worse crime standard, a worse set of schools, a worse circumstance to live in and work in than the city of Washington.

I do not care who knows it. I will tell everyone.

Mr. DOLE. The Senator already did.

> *—Sens. Ted Stevens (R-Alaska) and Robert Dole (R-Kans.)*
> *March 30, 1982*

SIT DOWN AND SHUT UP

Mr. ALLEN. Now, Mr. President, it occurs to the Senator from Alabama that this would be a far-reaching reform of Senate procedures, a reform that would revolutionize the legislative process here in the Senate Chamber, and would make of each of the Senators an equal. It would require the Senator to obtain his briefing from his staff, both present and anticipated, outside the Senate Chamber, and we would all come in here with such knowledge as we had acquired, and we could have some real debate at that time, and we would not have a 50-page text or prepared remarks that we would read from.

It would put everybody on exactly the same basis. We would not have these long-winded speeches, in my judgment. We would say what we had to say, and—

Mr. HUMPHREY. I say to the Senator, that would not stop me. [Laughter.]

Mr. ALLEN. We would say what we had to say and then we would sit down, which I am going to do at this time.

—Sens. James B. Allen (D-Ala.) and Hubert H. Humphrey (D-Minn.)
June 12, 1975

I CAN GO ON. IT GETS WORSE

Mr. NUNN. I am glad the Senator brought that up. I will get to it. The AWACS have the big orbits. With the E-2-C's, they would have to have 88. There are currently only 85 E-2-C's in the entire Navy. So we would have to bring all of them home.

In fact, this makes the Mansfield amendment look like an aggressive, forward defense strategy. We will have to bring everybody home. We will have to bring the Navy home, because they will not have surveillance.

Let me go forward and describe it a little further....

Mr. BIDEN. Mr. President, will the Senator yield for a question?

Mr. NUNN. I can go on. It gets worse.

Mr. BIDEN. I have been here with the Senator from Georgia as long as he has been here and having witnessed a number of debates, I never witnessed the moral equivalent of the requirement of surrender here.

Would the Senator from Georgia allow the rest of the Chamber to surrender and vote with him and get on with the vote? His case is so overwhelming, so compelling, I do not know how anyone could vote for it, although it is enjoyable to listen to it. I think maybe we could suggest the sponsor of the amendment bring the amendment down and we can go with the rest of this vote.

Mr. NUNN. Mr. President, let me just give you a couple more statistics.

Mr. BIDEN. The Senator does not want to surrender.

Mr. NUNN. It would take 800 helicopters.

Mr. BIDEN. What does it take to get the Senator to stop?

Mr. CHAFEE. Is the Senator prepared to take a few prisoners?

> —*Sens. Sam Nunn (D-Ga.), Joseph R. Biden, Jr. (D-Del.), and*
> *John H. Chafee (R-R.I.)*
> *September 27, 1986*

END OF THE ROAD

Mr. HUGH SCOTT. I am glad we are near the end of the road. So far as I am concerned it cannot come too soon for me. I hope we do not run into any more stop signs or that we have to yield for any pedestrian obfuscations on the part of well-intentioned colleagues.

I hope that the road ahead is clear, that there are no potholes in the immediate future, and that we can arrive at our destination together and united after an interesting exercise in very high-toned disagreement.

Mr. ABOUREZK. Futility. [Laughter.]

Mr. HUGH SCOTT. Not futility, as the Senator suggests, but a determination that howsoever one may have to use all of the rules of the Senate, and however long it takes that somehow we do arrive at this valued consensus at the end, and I thank all those who helped. I join in the general relief for the rest of the Senate who have had to listen to them.

Mr. ABOUREZK. Mr. President, after all of these speeches, I am not so sure that we would not have been better off to have gone on through in trying to shut off the debate. [Laughter.]

Mr. HUGH SCOTT. Why does not the Senator say encomia.

> —*Sens. Hugh Scott (R-Pa.) and James Abourezk (D-S.D.)*
> *June 10, 1976*

A LOT OF FINE RECIPES

Mr. BAKER. I thank the Senator from Arkansas....

I hope that the Senator from Arkansas will give me an opportunity to confer with the managers to see if we cannot address his questions and his problem. I recognize as a sister and adjoining State that there are problems unique to our region. For a moment there, I thought the Senator was going to talk about rice. But had I interjected that, I would have been wrong. I have not yet addressed the question of how bromine affects Arkansas, but I am prepared to do so.

Mr. PRYOR. The majority leader has just given the Senator from Arkansas an idea, and I might up end up doing that if there is a motion.

Mr. BAKER. I will never forgive myself for having opened my mouth.

Mr. PRYOR. We have a lot of fine recipes, as I recall.

Mr. BAKER. I do remember the Senator reading at length, and, indeed, the CONGRESSIONAL RECORD become a veritable compendium of recipes for ways to fix rice that ran to no doubt a thousand pages.

Mr. PRYOR. The best seller on that list was the rice recipe, as I recall, belonging to the wife of the very distinguished Senator from Louisiana, Senator LONG—Mrs. Carolyn Long. That recipe was the best seller, as I recall.

Mr. DANFORTH. Mr. President, let me say I understand the problem of the Senator from Arkansas, and I appreciate his problem. I am confident that there are ways to take care of the problem which will be totally satisfactory to him....I think we can provide about as close to an ironclad guarantee as possible that this problem will be taken care of to his satisfaction without the necessity of resorting to too many rice recipes.

—Sens. David Pryor (D-Ark.), Howard H. Baker, Jr. (R-Tenn.), and
John C. Danforth (R-Mo.)
September 19, 1984

STUFFING

Mr. RHODES. Mr. Speaker, I would like to take this occasion to wish the Speaker and the acting majority leader a very fine Thanksgiving and a restful and plentiful recess.

Mr. McFALL. If the gentleman will yield, I thank the gentleman. I wish the gentleman and all of the Members the same.

Mr. BAUMAN. Mr. Speaker, will the gentleman yield?

Mr. RHODES. I yield to the gentleman from Maryland.

Mr. BAUMAN. I thank the gentleman for yielding.

Mr. Speaker, I want to join in wishing the acting majority leader a fine vacation, and I would suggest if he has not ordered his turkey that he might want to take the New York bill home with him as a replacement.

Mr. McFALL. If the gentleman will yield, I appreciate the suggestion of the gentleman from Maryland, but it might be pretty hard for me to chew.

—Reps. John J. Rhodes (R-Ariz.), John J. McFall (D-Calif.), and Robert E. Bauman (R-Md.) November 20, 1975

RADIO DAYS

Mr. BLEASE. Now they want to put a radio back here right behind me so as to broadcast what is going on in the Senate. I do not know anything about radios; I never listened to one of them in my life. I do not know what they might do, and that is what I want to ask Senators. What danger might lurk in such an instrument, for instance, at the time of the inauguration, now only three days distant? They might fill that thing up with gas, some deadly gas, and just about the time the crowd assembled in this chamber, everybody in control of the government of the United States, some fellow might turn on a machine down here and just gas out the whole business.

I do not care very much about the radio bill. I will be honest about it. I am opposed to it. I was the only man who voted against it when it came up. I have rather peculiar ideas, I guess, and perhaps a lot of people think they are fool ideas. I suppose some would put a "d" in front of that word to better express the kind of ideas they think I have. But to save my life I can not see what right we have to control the air that God Almighty gave the people.

—Sen. Cole L. Blease (D-S.C.) March 1, 1929

WHATEVER BECAME OF THAT SWORD?

Mr. LONG. Here is a suggestion which has just come to me.

The VICE PRESIDENT. Does the Senator desire to make the suggestion public?

Mr. LONG. Yes. I shall not disclose any names. I have been asked to relate the history of Frederick the Great. [Laughter.]

Everybody remembers Frederick the Great. The things I have related about Frederick the Great have appealed to people, but the thing which appealed to most people was his taking of Vienna....

These are examples of Frederick the Great which I have discussed time after time. Frederick the Great had been recognized as the greatest general of Europe—that was the record he had. Soon thereafter, when George Washington became leader of the United States Revolutionary forces and accomplished the great victory, and when Cornwallis had laid down his arms at Yorktown, Frederick the Great sent his sword to Washington and sent a message to Washington in which he said, "I am sending the sword, given to me as the greatest general of Europe, to George Washington, the greatest general of the world." So among the treasures that George Washington had at his death was the sword which was sent to Washington by Frederick the Great.

I wonder whatever became of that sword? I wonder if that is in the Smithsonian Institution or if it is in some other historical museum? I have not taken the time to look that up. I should be very grateful to any of my friends if they could inform me what happened to the sword sent to George Washington by Frederick the Great. I should like to find out about it. I had intended some day to make a search here in Washington and see what became of that historic weapon.

The VICE PRESIDENT. Did the Senator make an inquiry of the Chair?

Mr. LONG. May I make that as a parliamentary inquiry?

The VICE PRESIDENT. Yes. The present occupant of the chair is very much surprised that the Senator from Louisiana does not have this information. He seems to have all other information and ought to have had at least this information. [Laughter.]

Mr. LONG. But I have not. By accident it happens to be one of the few things I have not yet dug up. That is why I was asking the Chair, who either knows or has a way of keeping everybody from knowing that he does not know what has happened to that sword which Frederick the Great sent to Washington. [Laughter.] I propounded that as a parliamentary inquiry in good faith. I should like to have it answered in some way by some of our statesman.

Mr. President, I shall have to ask for order in the Senate.

The VICE PRESIDENT. Senators will be in order, in order that the Senator from Louisiana may be heard by Senators in the Chamber.

Mr. LONG. It looks like two of my friends are double teaming on me.

Mr. BLACK. Mr. President, may I ask the Senator from Louisiana to speak a little louder.

The VICE PRESIDENT. The Senator from Louisiana will speak loud enough for Senators on the floor to hear and for the occupants of the gallery to hear. [Laughter.]

Mr. LONG. I shall undertake to do that. If the Senator from Alabama is complaining, I shall undertake to do that. I always did know he was hard of hearing, not that there is anything wrong with his ears, but he cannot even hear what comes into his ears. There are none so deaf as those who, having ears, hear not, and none so blind as those who, having eyes, see not. The Senator falls in that category—blind, deaf, and dumb. He does not want to be any other way, either. He did not hear what I said.

Mr. BLACK. Speak a little louder.

Mr. LONG. I was telling about Frederick the Great sending his sword to George Washington, and I propounded a parliamentary inquiry to the Chair, whether the Chair knew what became of the sword sent by Frederick the Great to George Washington. The Chair never did say. The Senator from Alabama could go out and dig up that information for me in a few moments if he had a mind to do it, and I could put it in the RECORD right now.

What became of the sword sent by Frederick the Great to Gen. George Washington? That is the question I invoke before the Senate now. Where did it go? That is what I am trying to find out.

Mr. McKELLAR. Perhaps one of the Senator's bodyguards up in the gallery has it.

> —*Sens. Huey P. Long (D-La.), Hugo Black (D-Ala.), and*
> *Kenneth D. McKellar (D-Tenn.)*
> *June 13, 1935*

CAPITOL
PUNISHMENT

A bit of seven-upsmanship

CAPITOL
PUNISHMENT

DRINK IT UP

Mr. HUGH SCOTT. I have often observed during my service here that the members of my party are totally unable to outbid the opposition, because whatever figure I suggest will immediately be not one-upped but two-upped, or even seven-upped on the other side. This is refreshing and spritely.

[Laughter.]

I often wonder what they gain by this other than the fact that we have been sort of charged up.

Mr. ROBERT C. BYRD. It is the pause that refreshes.

[Laughter.]

— Sens. Hugh Scott (R-Pa.) and Robert C. Byrd (D-W. Va.)
October 10, 1974

TWO IN THE BUSH

Mr. BYRD. Will the Senator yield?

Mr. QUAYLE. I yield to the Senator from West Virginia, who is a cosponsor of the amendment.

Mr. BYRD. Mr. President, I very much support the amendment. I am happy to be a cosponsor.

Almost as long as I have been in the Senate there have been two "birds" in the Senate. There are still two "birds" in the Senate. One is a "Quayle" and the other is a "Byrd."

I compliment the Senator strongly and I do hope the amendment is agreed to.

Mr. QUAYLE. I thank the Senator. I might say that I am a proud member of the "bird caucus."

Mr. President, I yield the floor.

—Sens. Robert C. Byrd (D-W. Va.) and Dan Quayle (R-Ind.)
November 7, 1983

FOWL PLAY

Mr. HOWE. Mr. Speaker, I note that our distinguished majority leader, the Honorable TIP O'NEILL, recently cried "foul" at President Ford's attempt to pluck at the emotions of the people by calling the Congress "chicken."

I, too, would like to object to this attempt by the President to duck his own responsibility by trying to make it appear that the Members of Congress have egg on their faces. I think the Members of this distinguished body have a lot to crow about.

The President, evidently, would like the Congress to take under its wing every scheme he hatches and make it work. But this Congress, fortunately, has not been content to follow the President's rather scrambled approach to solving this Nation's problems. Not that we are hardboiled about it—when the President has proposed good programs this Congress has not been reluctant to pronounce them "Grade A" and pass them. But, frankly, very often when the President proposes a program, he simply lays an egg. If this Congress had passed some of the President's programs that were obviously doomed to failure, we would now be in the position of having to recoup our losses.

But this Congress has worked and is working hard at good solutions to America's problems—we have taken up the yoke and we are rolling along toward responsible programs.

Some people may charge that the progress of Congress toward solutions to such problems as the economy and energy is so slow, that the

Congress is working by the hunt and peck method. But, if it is true that we are pecking away at problems and that we sometimes seem to be scratching around for ideas, it is equally true that this Congress is taking such a slow and deliberate course of action in order to make sure that in curing our Nation's ills, we do not kill the goose that lays the golden egg by attempting to gain too much too soon. Of course, we cannot brood over problems forever, and I do not think this Congress has.

The President's charges against Congress are, in my opinion, simply a politically motivated attempt to feather his own nest. But, I think the people of America will soon come to realize this, and then the chickens will come home to roost.

— Rep. Allan T. Howe (D-Utah)
September 23, 1975

GIVE A DAM

Mr. HUNGATE. Mr. Speaker, if someone would like to see the gentleman who has the dam in this district, look here. I am disappointed. The gentleman from Illinois said some feel strongly about this. I do not feel strongly about this. Some feel strongly about this. I think it is a good idea, and necessary. I am disappointed that my colleague from Illinois would oppose a dam in my district. I would be willing to dam his district at any time....

While talking about that 12-foot channel and the dam—you know that while you always find a dam by a mill site, you do not always find a mill by a damn site.

— Rep. William L. Hungate (D-Mo.)
May 22, 1975

**THE
GREATEST
SHOW
ON EARTH,
ALMOST**

Tales from the two-ring circus

THE
GREATEST
SHOW
ON EARTH,
ALMOST

EXCUSES

Mr. McGEE. Mr. President, I wanted to make perfectly clear for the RECORD, in view of the remarks here this morning, that I am not here as a reluctant participant on this Saturday session. My colleague and I, if we could only be in Wyoming, would have many other things that would be far more delightful than spending Saturday in this way, as he suggested.

But I have to confess, since we are here, that I was scheduled to mow the lawn today and to go after the crab grass in my lawn, and that I am here hiding out, as it were. I would hope that the leadership would be able to keep us until dark tonight, and I will follow the leadership in the pursuit of the business of the day and will stand ready to cooperate in every way.

Mr. ROBERT C. BYRD. Mr. President, I am sorry that I cannot assure the distinguished Senator from Wyoming that the leadership will keep us here until dark.

Mr. McGEE. Well, if the Senator will make it appear that I was here until dark, then.

[Laughter.]

—Sens. Gale W. McGee (D-Wyo.) and Robert C. Byrd (D-W. Va.)
July 19, 1975

COLD COMFORT

The ACTING PRESIDENT pro tempore (Mr. HEFLIN). The Chair would like the Sergeant at Arms to bring forth the official Senate thermometer. [Laughter.]

Mr. LEAHY. Mr. President, this would be considered a heat wave in Vermont. I find it very comfortable here in the Chamber. I know in the few years I have been here it seems often that the Senate Chamber is chilled almost unbearably during the summer and heated unbearably during the winter. Now we seem finally to have moved it around the other way. I just assumed under one of the special orders that the temperature was just dropped to make me feel a lot more comfortable.

Mr. STEVENS. Mr. President, will the Senator yield?

Mr. LEAHY. I yield to the Senator from Alaska.

Mr. STEVENS. I was just admiring the majority leader's sweater and vest today, and thought this was a great temperature. I would urge the present occupant of the chair to obtain the thermometer and see if we cannot come to an accord that, perhaps, this is the time of year to visit his part of the country and enjoy the warmth and hospitality and spirit of the South. But this is a very comfortable Chamber for an Alaskan Senator.

Mr. LEAHY. I must admit that it is comfortable for a Vermonter as well.

The ACTING PRESIDENT pro tempore. The Chair cannot help but observe that the Senator from Vermont's hands have been in his pockets most of the time. [Laughter.]

Mr. ROBERT C. BYRD. Mr. President, the chill falls alike on the just and unjust. The important thing is to keep the temperature down, be well-clothed, and conserve energy.

—*Sens. Howell Heflin (D-Ala.), Patrick J. Leahy (D-Vt.), Ted Stevens (R-Alaska), and Robert C. Byrd (D-W. Va.) January 31, 1980*

HIGH TECH

Mr. MUSKIE. I wish to make a unanimous-consent request, the necessity for which I find incredible. I ask unanimous consent to use hand calculators on the Senate floor.

The PRESIDING OFFICER (Mr. FORD). Without objection, it is so ordered.

Mr. MUSKIE. I understand that the rules are so ancient and esoteric that the ability to use these calculators except by unanimous consent seems to be in doubt. I asked whether or not I could use my fingers without unanimous consent—I assume that that is the original hand calculator—and there seems to be some doubt on that score, too.

—Sen. Edmund S. Muskie (D-Maine)
April 29, 1975

HOT SEATS

Mr. SIKES. Mr. Chairman, I offer an amendment which is at the Clerk's desk.

The Clerk read as follows:

Amendment offered by Mr. SIKES: On page 2, lines 14 and 15, strike out the words "Furniture: For an additional amount for 'Furniture', $58,750, to remain available until June 30, 1954, and."

Mr. SIKES. Mr. Chairman, this is not a major item. Fifty-eight thousand seven hundred and fifty dollars cannot be called a lot of money to a Congress which has become accustomed to dealing in billions.

But, Mr. Chairman, this is a touchy item. This could become the hottest potato in this session of Congress. It could even be called a matter of principle, because we are speaking of balancing the budget and we are talking about reducing taxes.... Mr. Chairman, we propose to vote for the Congress new chairs, which already are referred to by press and radio commentators as "fancy chairs" and "luxury seats." We propose also to vote for new carpets. We can get along very well with the chairs and carpets we now have and in truth most of us have not requested and do not want new furniture....

Mr. BENDER. Mr. Chairman, I move to strike out the last word.

Mr. Chairman, I do not know how much money was required to modernize the House Chamber and the Chamber of the other body. It seemed to me that the chairs we had before the renovation were very comfortable; in any event, it was determined to change the whole works. No question was raised regarding that and I am sure the cost ran into the millions.

This country wants Congressmen with backbone. My medical friends both inside and outside the AMA tell me that the best way to acquire a backbone if you do not have one or to retain it if you do is to stand up straight whenever you are sitting down. There is no sense in using the fine, comfortable 1953 model chairs we have in the House Chamber a few hours daily if we must go back to offices equipped with 1853 horsehair torture chairs.

I think the country will receive a net gain in service with these good chairs instead of those a few dollars cheaper. Far more expensive legislation will be passed by back-weary Congressmen who cannot stand up to pressure groups because they can scarcely stand up at all than by the fine specimen of upstanding Congressmen whose backs are models of orthopedic virtue....

While we are discussing corrective measures for the Capitol and House Office Buildings, I wish someone would offer an amendment to spend $50,000 or whatever amount is required to get the cockroaches out of this building and the New and Old House Office Buildings. These pests become so numerous at times that we should take drastic steps to exterminate them. And while we are doing a clean-up job let us not overlook the restaurant downstairs....

Mr. MAHON. Mr. Chairman, will the gentleman yield?

Mr. BENDER. I yield to the gentleman from Texas.

Mr. MAHON. In all seriousness, I think any Member is entitled to any kind of a chair he wants within the bounds of reason. However, there are some of us who prefer those old chairs, and we do not want these new ones to be inflicted upon us. I wonder if it would not be wise for the gentleman from Florida [Mr. SIKES] to modify his amendment, cutting it in half, so that those of us who want the old ones may have them and those who want the new ones may also have them?

Mr. BENDER. As far as I am concerned, if you want to sit on the floor that is perfectly all right with me....

Mr. SHAFER. Mr. Chairman, will the gentleman yield?

Mr. BENDER. I yield to the gentleman from Michigan.

Mr. SHAFER. Is there any truth in the report I hear that those boys who want these high back chairs all have weak backs?

Mr. BENDER. Maybe the gentleman has something there.

The CHAIRMAN. The question is on the amendment offered by the gentleman from Florida [Mr. SIKES].

The question was taken; and on a division (demanded by Mr. SIKES) there were—ayes 42, noes 117.

So the amendment was rejected.

— Reps. Robert L.F. (Bob) Sikes (D-Fla.), George H. Bender (R-Ohio), George H. Mahon (D-Tex.), and Paul W. Shafer (R-Mich.)
February 26, 1953

EARTHY

Mr. GROSS. I have no desire or intent to hold up pay increases for Federal employees, particularly at this time of year.

However, Mr. Speaker, at the roots of this Christmas tree is a great big can of worms.

— Rep. H.R. Gross (R-Neb.)
December 11, 1967

FLOOD WARNING

Mr. FLOOD. Mr. Chairman, as usual—and believe me, when I say "as usual" I mean as usual, and the Members serve on all kinds of committees and they think they have problems, they think they have difficulties; but if a Member has ever gotten mixed up with a can of worms he ought to sit with us on the Labor-Health, Education, and Welfare Subcommittee. They ought to spend a week with us. Ay, yi, yi....

The reason we brought up this bill now for education appropriations is to get it through early so the people back home can get their money for educational planning as quickly as possible. This is the time to do it, early in the year.

If we fool around with this thing, we are going to get a veto right between the eyes, and there goes the whole purpose for an early education appropriations bill; we would destroy the whole purpose and the whole intent of it right there.

Now, if you want to go back home and see your school directors after that happens, this is what they would tell you: "Why didn't you pass that bill you were talking about? He told you not to add to this thing; he told you to leave it alone; he told you it would be vetoed. Now it is vetoed and kicked around, and here it is 7 months later and we don't know where it is. It is your fault. You can look right in the CONGRESSIONAL RECORD."

So let us skip the telegrams and the telephone calls. Just listen to FLOOD, and you will wear diamonds.

—Rep. Daniel J. Flood (D-Pa.)
April 16, 1975

VOICE OF REASON

Mr. LEVIN. Mr. President, I understand that the squawkboxes are not working and that they are playing music instead of my melodious voice.

I ask unanimous consent that I may suggest the absence of a quorum and that the time for that quorum not be charged to either side, to give the engineers an opportunity to fix our squawkboxes.

—Sen. Carl Levin (D-Mich.)
November 6, 1985

BLACK-AND-WHITE ISSUE

Mr. GROSS. Mr. Speaker, if the gentleman will yield, does the gentleman know whether we will have these floodlights on, and that we will have to live with those floodlights on for some 24 hours a day?

Mr. LATTA. The question arose at the time of the hearings before the Committee on the Judiciary being televised as to whether or not the lights would be on high for them, or on dim. If you want to appear in color you will have to have the bright lights.

Mr. GROSS. I do not care to appear in living color.

> *—Reps. H.R. Gross (R-Iowa) and Delbert L. Latta (R-Ohio)*
> *August 7, 1974*

TIE VOTE

Mr. DOLE. Will the Senator from Massachusetts yield for a question?

Mr. TSONGAS. I yield.

Mr. DOLE. The Senator from Kansas is curious: Had we authorized television in the Senate earlier this year, would all this be on television?

Mr. TSONGAS. I say to the Senator that it would be, but we would be dressed differently. There would be more red ties and blue shirts than is now the case.

Mr. DOLE. If ever a case is made for no television in the Senate, we have done it today. [Laughter.]

Mr. STEVENS. Is the Senator talking about my tie?

> *—Sens. Robert Dole (R-Kans.) Paul E. Tsongas (D-Mass.), and*
> *Ted Stevens (R-Alaska)*
> *March 30, 1982*

FOOD FIGHT

Mr. HUMPHREY. Mr. President, coming on the heels of the 5.5 percent pay raise for Federal workers is an increase of 25 percent and more in the price of food served in the Senate cafeterias. I question this method of taking back the pay increase for Senate employees.

While McDonalds is selling its hamburgers for 30 cents, it will cost you

75 cents—up from 60 cents—to get a similar one at a Senate cafeteria. The House of Representatives cafeteria manages, somehow, to sell the same hamburger for 50 cents. Cheeseburgers in the Senate are 95 cents, and in the House cafeteria they are 65 cents. At McDonalds, cheeseburgers are 37 cents. A bowl of soup will be 45 cents in the Senate—up from 35 cents.

Mr. President, I wish the dairy farmers in Minnesota could share in the Senate's profit from milk. A one-half pint carton of milk goes for 25 cents. That amounts to $1 a quart, or $4 per gallon.

The price of chili rose better than 30 percent—from 65 to 85 cents. Over on the House side, where prices have not gone up, chili goes for 55 cents.

Both Houses' cafeterias are supposedly run on purely a self-sustaining, and not a profitmaking basis.

Mr. President, I do not understand how the House cafeteria is able to operate effectively with an overall 25 percent lower cost to the employees who eat there. The price difference surely could not result from the difference in the quality of the food. The quality of the food served in the Senate—especially in the snack bar in the Russell Office Building—is quite another matter.

I am hopeful that consideration will be given toward reversing this inflationary move.

Mr. President, I ask unanimous consent to have printed in the RECORD a chart showing the old and new prices for selected items sold in the Senate cafeteria and comparing these with prices in the House cafeteria.

There being no objection, the chart was ordered to be printed in the RECORD, as follows:

SENATE AND HOUSE CAFETERIA PRICES

	Old Senate price	House price	New Senate price
Soup	0.35	0.35	0.45
Cottage cheese	.25	.25	.25
Cottage cheese and fruit	.60	.55	.70
Hamburger	.60	.50	.75
Cheeseburger	.80	.65	.95
Chili	.65	.55	.85
French fries	.35	.30	.45

SENATE AND HOUSE CAFETERIA PRICES

	Old Senate price	House price	New Senate price
Hot dog	.40	.40	.50
Milk	.20	.20	.25
Grilled cheese	.35	.50	.50
Grilled ham and cheese	1.10	1.00	1.30
Grilled bacon and cheese	.80	.70	.90
Grilled tomato and cheese	.80	.55	.90
Ham and cheese sandwich	1.10	.80	1.30
Pudding	.25	.25	.25
Crackers	.05	.03	.05
Lettuce wedge	.35	.35	.50
Lettuce and sliced tomato	.35	.35	.50
Tossed salad	.35	.30	.50
Milk shake	.40	.35	.45
Cake	.30	.25	.35
Ice cream (per scoop)	.20	.30	.25
Bacon (per slice)	.15	.15	.20
Sausage	.20	.35	.25

*Figures supplied by House and Senate cafeterias.

— *Sen. Hubert H. Humphrey (D-Minn.)*
October 2, 1974

CIVIL WAR REDUX

Mr. DOWNEY of New York. Mr. Speaker, I just have one question. I am very curious about one matter. Very probably the gentleman from Virginia could answer my question. Does this restore General Lee's right to hold elective office in the United States?

Mr. HARRIS. Mr. Speaker, will the gentleman yield?

Mr. DOWNEY of New York. I yield to the gentleman from Virginia.

Mr. HARRIS. I thank the gentleman for yielding.

The rights of returned citizenship under the laws and Constitution of the United States restore General Lee's right to hold elective office, although I do not fear any campaign threat next year.

> — *Reps. Thomas J. Downey (D-N.Y.) and Herbert E. Harris II (D-Va.)*
> *July 22, 1975*

DRESS CODE

Mrs. SCHROEDER. Mr. Speaker, I have a question which I would like to pose here to the gentleman from Indiana (Mr. JACOBS), whom I see on the floor. Therefore, I take this time to ask him about this particular question. I know he has been very worried about the matter of a dress code for the Members of the House and whether it should apply equally to both men and women.

Mr. Speaker, I think he may be pleased or may not be pleased to find out that the President has picked up his cause, and as a consequence, has caused me a great problem.

I have correspondence from the President of the United States saying that if I wished to ride on Air Force One to Denver, Colo., tomorrow, I would have to wear a business suit, and I do not have one.

Mr. Speaker, I was wondering whether, if the gentleman from Indiana (Mr. JACOBS) feels strong about a uniform dress code for both sexes, he would be able to find me a business suit for tomorrow afternoon.

Mr. JACOBS. If the gentlewoman will yield, Mr. Speaker, I would suggest to the gentlewoman that I do own one suit, but it is not a spring suit. Also, in the event there was some trouble on the flight requiring a parachute, I would suggest that the gentlewoman wear a spring suit to cushion the fall, or, if the gentlewoman needed a scarf, I would refer her to the Honorable Snoopy.

> — *Reps. Patricia Schroeder (D-Colo.) and Andrew Jacobs, Jr. (D-Ind.)*
> *May 2, 1978*

WILL THE GENTLEMAN WAIT?

Mr. DOLE. Mr. President, will the Senator yield?

Mr. BIDEN. Yes.

Mr. DOLE. Has the Senator been to a party, or do you have a part-time job? [Laughter.]

Mr. BIDEN. Mr. President, I believe I have the floor and I am happy to answer the question.

After we get finished with these amendments, I am going to need this uniform so that I get a job as a headwaiter in order to be able to make it.

—*Sens. Robert Dole (R-Kans.) and Joseph R. Biden, Jr. (D-Del.)*
March 30, 1982

DO YOU KNOW ME?

Mr. BAKER. Mr. President, this is the first week of summer. I do not clearly recall if we had any spring. In any event, it is nice to know that summer has arrived and with it, inevitably, the realization that we go downhill from here, as the days grow shorter from this day forward until mid-December.

Mr. President, it also means that the Capitol Building, to say nothing of the city as a whole, will look forward to the visitation of countless millions of visitors.

I always count it a great tribute to the solidity and future of American democracy that so many Americans want to come to this city and see the monumental structures, the Capitol, the White House, the Mall, and to travel through those spaces, including the corridors of the Capitol Building itself.

Sometimes the throng of tourists through the Capitol corridors can become an impediment to progress. Sometimes, even, it can be an assault on one's ego.

The other day, I was walking from this Chamber back to my office, and an excited group stopped me and someone said, "Say, I know who you are. Don't tell me. Let me guess. Let me remember. I'll get it in a minute."

I waited for several seconds, and finally I said, "Howard Baker"; and he said, "No, that's not it." [Laughter.]

— Sen. Howard H. Baker, Jr. (R-Tenn.)
June 23, 1983

THE TWO-SECOND SENATE

The Senate met at 9 o'clock a.m., and was called to order by the acting President pro tempore [Mr. METCALF].

The ACTING PRESIDENT pro tempore. Under previous order, the Senate will now adjourn to 10 a.m. Monday next.

ADJOURNMENT TO MONDAY, DECEMBER 30, 1963

Thereupon (at 9 o'clock and 2 seconds a.m.) the Senate adjourned, under the order of Tuesday, December 24, 1963, until Monday, December 30, 1963, at 10 o'clock a.m.

— December 27, 1963

PROUD PAPA

Mr. BAKER. Mr. President, I am happy to report to my colleagues that the distinguished assistant Republican leader, Senator STEVENS, and his wife Catherine are the proud parents of a new baby girl. Both baby and mother are reportedly doing fine, and as far as we can ascertain, so is Senator STEVENS.

Senator STEVENS' daughter, who will be named later today, was born at 12:08 this morning at George Washington University Hospital.

It is truly a touching sight, Mr. President, to see a proud papa gallivanting through the Capitol corridors with a smile on his face and a box of cigars in his hand. Even more touching is the conversation that corners

Senator STEVENS with polemics on reconciliation, and finishes with "and she looks just like me."

I am sure that I speak for this entire body in wishing the new parents all the very best for their entire family....

Mr. MURKOWSKI....Mr. President, in the finest traditions of the Republican leadership, this is the first baby born to a Republican Member of the 97th Congress. Not only is TED now my colleague, but my longtime friend, as are members of both our families. Mrs. Murkowski and I and delighted at this new addition to the Stevens family, and I am sure that other Members of the Senate join me in extending warm congratulations to them.

I might mention that my colleague is said to be currently in a state of shock over the price increase of a box of cigars in the last 25 years.

Mr. DOLE. I thank the distinguished Senator from Alaska. We will accept the addition. [Laughter.]

— Sens. Howard H. Baker, Jr. (R-Tenn.), Frank H. Murkowski (R-Alaska), and
Robert Dole (R-Kans.)
July 23, 1981

UPS AND DOWNS

Mr. JACOBS. Mr. Speaker, after careful and scholarly study I have concluded that the principal cause of congressional inefficiency is the elevator system in the Longworth Building.

— Rep. Andrew Jacobs, Jr. (D-Ind.)
June 15, 1976

HARD ROCK

Mr. BAUCUS. Another minor problem in the use of physical space of congressional facilities is the inner courtyard in the Cannon and Longworth Buildings. It puzzles me how Congress can pass laws promoting a better use of the environment and then keep its own physical facilities in such a stark manner. When I return from a vote on the floor, I find it unpleasant to closet myself in an office overlooking the gray, grim space that is the inner courtyard in Cannon. To say that our courtyards resemble Attica or Sing-Sing may not be much of an exaggeration. Actually, it might be an improvement to see people breaking rocks in the Cannon courtyard as, indeed, any sign of life would be better than the lifeless view we now have.

— Rep. Max Baucus (D-Mont.)
April 27, 1976

BUGGED

Mr. LONG. Mr. President, answering the question which has been propounded by my friend from Nevada, it is my belief, as a very close student of the Constitution and of constitutional questions, as one who has given hours of time to reading the Constitution and reading the debates over and about the Constitution by Madison and by Hamilton, by Patrick Henry and by James Monroe, as one who has studied diligently into constitutional history and the arguments pro and con affecting the Constitution, I state—Mr. President, what is that bug that just lit on my arm? At least I ought to be protected from the annoyance of bugs. [Laughter.]

Mr. McCARRAN. Mr. President, will the Senator yield?

Mr. LONG. I yield for a question.

Mr. McCARRAN. By any chance could that have been a chinch bug?

Mr. LONG. It looked like a chinch bug to me, very much like a chinch bug. [Laughter.] That is what I thought it was, as a matter of fact. It came in here and attacked me! [Laughter.]

— Sens. Huey P. Long (D-La.) and Pat McCarran (D-Nev.)
June 13, 1935

NO SENSE

Mr. PRYOR submitted the following resolution; which was referred to the Committee on Rules and Administration:

RESOLUTION
S. RES. 194
Relative to Sense of the Senate resolutions.

Resolved, That it is the sense of the Senate that there be no more "sense of the Senate" resolutions.

—Sen. David Pryor (D-Ark.)
July 23, 1981

A LOTTA BULL

Mr. HUGH SCOTT. We have already, at my suggestion, agreed to go right ahead with the suggestion of the Senator from Arkansas (Mr. McCLEL-LAN). But it would not be in order to ask the minority leader whether he would let the Senate operate. That is a good deal like asking the bull whether he will let the cows come into the pasture. I think it is a matter within the bull's discretion as to what he does with the cows, and what the bull has been doing with the cows lately is a shame.

Mr. MANSFIELD. Who are the cows?

Mr. HUGH SCOTT. I think I will leave that to the distinguished majority leader.

—Sens. Hugh Scott (R-Pa.) and Mike Mansfield (D-Mont.)
July 16, 1975

SHORT SUBJECTS

Mr. TOWER. It is an anachronism, I suppose, in the context of this time, that the Senator from Texas represents 12 million people and has one vote in the Senate, and the Senator from Rhode Island represents 1.5 million people and has one vote in the Senate. I submit that that in itself is an anachronism....

Mr. PASTORE. Will the Senator yield?

Mr. TOWER. I yield.

Mr. PASTORE. It is true that the Senator has a lot more people in Texas than we have in Rhode Island, but is it not remarkable and marvelous that the Senator and I are about the same size? [Laughter.]

Mr. TOWER. I agree.

Mr. President, I was only making the observation that I am atypical, and that Senator PASTORE is not because he is a Rhode Island-size Rhode Islander and I am a Rhode Island-size Texan.

[Laughter.]

—Sens. John Tower (R-Tex.) and John O. Pastore (D-R.I.)
February 20, 1975

CMDR. CORNHUSKER

Mr. DOWNEY. Mr. Speaker, some time ago an Army general of White House position and absurd twist of mind delivered himself of some spectacularly bizarre remarks on the state of the U.S. military posture. I then took the well of the House and remarked, among other things, that this gentleman could, even in this administration, expect transfer to command of all submarines in the Nebraska National Guard.

As it turns out, I was speaking from abysmal ignorance, for which I hereby apologize with all due abjectness. The appropriate agency was not the Nebraska National Guard but the Great Navy of the State of Nebraska.

Upon reading of my interest in the subject, and of my passionate dedication to the security of the Nebraska sea lanes, the citizens of that great State have responded in a most heart warming and spine-tingling fashion.

To wit, they have appointed me an admiral in their great navy. For the benefit of any doubters and scoffers, I hold here in my hand the official commission and appointment, signed by the Governor himself.

While there may be some question as to the appropriateness of the rank involved, on the whole I believe it is the proper way to go. By not providing me with five-star rank immediately, the good citizens of Nebraska have permitted me room for growth.

Mr. Speaker, henceforth I will be honored to regard Nebraska as my second home. If I am to command anybody's navy, it is certainly best that it be that of the people of Nebraska, and I humbly hope I will continue to merit their confidence.

THE GREAT NAVY OF THE STATE OF NEBRASKA
TO ALL WHO SHALL SEE THESE PRESENTS—GREETINGS

Know ye, that reposing special trust and confidence in the Patriotism, valor, fidelity and abilities of Thomas Downey and knowing him to be a good fellow and a loyal friend and counselor I have nominated and do appoint him an Admiral in the Great Navy of the State of Nebraska. He is therefore called to diligently discharge the duties of Admiral by doing and performing all manner of things thereto belonging. And I do strictly charge and require all officers, seamen, tadpoles and goldfish under his command to be obedient to his orders as Admiral—and he is to observe and follow, from time to time, such directions as he shall receive, according to the rules and discipline of the Great Navy of the State of Nebraska. This commission to continue in good force during the period of his good behavior, and the pleasure of the Chief Admiral of the Great Navy of the State of Nebraska.

Given under my hand in the City of Lincoln, State of Nebraska this 4 day of November 1981 in the year of our Lord.

CHARLES THONE,
Governor.

— Rep. Thomas J. Downey (D-N.Y.)
December 15, 1981

PLASTIC FANTASTIC

Mr. MOYNIHAN submitted the following resolution; which was referred to the Committee on Rules and Administration:

S. RES. 140

Whereas in the Fall of 1980 the frame of the new Senate Office Building was covered with plastic sheathing in order that construction might continue during the winter months; and

Whereas the plastic cover has now been removed revealing, as feared, a building whose banality is exceeded only by its expense; and

Whereas, even in a democracy there are things it is as well the people do not know about their government;

Therefore, be it resolved, That it is the sense of the Senate that the plastic cover be put back.

—Sen. Daniel Patrick Moynihan (D-N.Y.)
May 19, 1981

INDEX OF NAMES

INDEX
OF
NAMES